.The 비로자나불
Vairocana

The Vairocana 毘盧遮那佛
비로자나불

비로자나불! 부처님의 무구한 진리 자체가 법신임을 확신하게 하며 소우주의 위대한 즉신성불임이 분명하다. 비로자나 부처님은 숲에서 나무를 찾고 바다에서 물을 찾는 중생들에게 마치 사바세계에 떠오르는 태양과 어두운 밤에 밝은 보름달과 같이 언제 어디서나 비추지 아니함이 없다.

Editor Jongil ; Translator Choonki, Park, Ph.D.

종일 편저 | **박춘기 영역**

은주사

나주 불회사 건칠비로자나불상

지권인은 부처와 중생이 하나임을 뜻하며, 건칠불상은 종이로 만들어 옻칠을 하고 다시 금물을 입힌 불상으로 고려말(1400년경)에 만들어졌다 (보물 제1545호).

추천의 글

한마음 청정하면
비로자나 부처님 나투시고

한마음 올바르면
비로자나 부처님 가호 있으시다

한마음 그 한마음은
우주가 생기기 이전에도 있었거니와
우주가 멸하더라도 있는 것이다

그러나 그 한마음 있음을 모르고
살아가는 게 중생이다
안타깝고 안타까운 일이다

하지만

인연이 있고 선근이 있는 이들은
본래 가지고 있는 청정법신 비로자나불을
체득할 수 있나니

청정법신 비로자나 부처님을
체득함으로써 우리네 삶이
영원히 나고 죽음에 벗어나
윤회의 수레바퀴에서 벗어날 수 있다
그리고 참된 자유 참된 행복을
영원토록 누릴 수 있다
이 얼마나 숭고한 이치인가

종일스님이 스스로 비로자나 부처님의
가호를 느끼고 법보시하고자
발원하므로 기쁘게 동참하나이다

불교TV 회장 석성우 합장

한글본 비로자나불 The Vairocana 毘盧遮那佛

추천의 글 — 7

머리말 — 13

서문 — 21

제1장 비로자나불의 위신력 — 25

제2장 비로자나불 십신불 — 35

제3장 법신불 — 39

제4장 보신불 — 42

제5장 응화불 — 43

제6장 법신불의 본유 — 45

제7장 진언밀교 불신관 — 48

제8장 법신불의 체상용 — 51

제9장 당체법문 — 54

제10장 육대무애 — 56

제11장 삼밀가지속질현 — 60

제12장 자성법신 — 63

제13장 현교와 밀교 — 65

제14장 현교와 밀교도 하나 불교 — 69

제15장 화엄사상에서 비로자나불 — 71

제16장 화엄세계 — 82

제17장 비로자나불상과 전각명 — 84

참고문헌 — 86

The Vairocana

영어본 비로자나불

Preface — 89

Introduction — 101

I. The Vairocana and His Power — 104
II. The Vairocana-10 Aspects of His Buddhakāya — 114
III. The *Dharmakāya-Buddha* — 120
IV. The *Sambhokāya* (*Rocana*) — 123
V. The *Nirmānakāya* (*Shakyamuni*)-the Transformed Buddhakāya — 125
VI. The Originality of the *Dharmakāya-Buddha* — 128
VII. Buddhist's View on the Theory of Esoteric Holy Words — 133
VIII. The Substance, Characteristics, and Function of the *Dharmakāya-Buddha* — 137
IX. The *Dharmakāya-Buddha* as Present Body and Mind — 141
X. The 6 Great Unimpeded Meta-Elements of Humanity and Universe — 145
XI. Becoming a Buddha Rapidly by Three Mystic Meta-Elements (Sammilgalgisokgilhyeun) — 149
XII. The *Sabhava Dharmakāya* — 156
XIII. The Written Holy Words and the Esoteric Holy Words — 157
XIV. The Theory of the Written Holy Words and the Esoteric Holy Words as One Buddhism — 162
XV. The *Variocana* Shown in the *Avatamsaka Sūtraism* (Whaom *Sūtra*: Whaomism in Korean) — 165
XVI. *Avatamaka Sūtra* World — 181
XVII. The *Vairocana* Statue and His Hall — 183

References — 186

Index — 191

한글본 毘盧遮那佛
비로자나불

The Vairocana in Korean

머리말

산중에서 비로자나[1] 부처님에 귀의歸依한 지 어언 40여 년을 지나고 보니, 사바세계娑婆世界에서 함께 살아가고 있는 생의 동반자인 일반인에게도 비로자나불의 소중한 법문法門을 알리고 싶은 마음이 일어난다. 물론, 언어·문자 여읜 우주의 청정법신淸淨法身인 비로자나 부처님의 참 진리를 문자로 표현하는 것은 쉽지가 않다. 산사에서 생활한 소승의 언어 표현능력 부족 또한 많은 걸림돌로 작용하고 있다. 그렇지만 거룩한 부처님의 말씀과 공덕功德을 전하는 일은 더욱

---

1 **비로자나**毘盧遮那는 부처님의 진신眞身을 나타내는 칭호인 산스크리트어 Vairocana를 음역한 것으로, 비로사나·비로절나毘嚧折那·폐로차나吠嚧遮那·노사나盧舍那·자나遮那 등으로 부르기도 하고, 또는 변일체처遍一切處·광명변조光明遍照·변조遍照로 의역하기도 한다.

원대하고 중차대한 일이라 생각하여 큰 발심發心을 내기로 하였다.

그동안 부족한 소승을 인도해주시고 자비慈悲와 광명을 함께 주신 비로자나 부처님과 바르게 이끌어주신 은사스님과 주위 선·후배, 그리고 수행의 길을 함께 해온 도반導伴들의 도움으로, 용기를 내어 한글본[2]과 영어본[3] 법문집을 집필하기로 하였다.

사실, 비로자나불은 '참 나'를 찾게 해주시고 성불成佛하게 이끌어주시는 법신 부처님이시다. 고통苦痛이나 극락極樂과 관계없이, 언제 어느 곳에서나 마음이 청정하면 부처님이 나타나신다고 한다.

---

[2] 한글본의 제3장부터 제14장까지 경의 내용은 현대 어법과는 다소 차이가 있지만, 독송하기 쉽게 4언절구四言絶句에 맞춘 표현임을 밝힌다.
[3] 영어본英語本은 외국인이 청정법신 비로자나 부처님을 이해할 수 있도록 도울 목적으로 편찬하였다.

인류가 오랜 기간 살아온 농경사회에서 산업사회로 전환되면서, 특히 21세기에 들어와서는 물질만능주의 사상이 더욱 팽배하여, 사람이 소우주라는 깊은 뜻을 잘 알지 못하고 대우주의 일부인 지구환경을 엄청나게 훼손하고 파괴하여, 지구 곳곳에 시시각각으로 각종 재앙들이 발생하고 있다. 자연을 훼손하여 세계 곳곳에서 홍수와 기후 온난화 등의 과보果報를 받고 있으며, 사랑과 박애 및 봉사를 부르짖는 종교인들조차 자기 국가의 영토 확장과 이익을 추구하기 위하여 끊임없이 전쟁 등을 일삼고 있다. 그리고 지식인들은 생·노·병·사生老病死에 대한 해결책과 현실의 행복마저 잘 알지 못하면서 잘난 체하며, 착하고, 성실하며, 못가진 사람들을 짓밟는 안하무인격의 무자비한 사람들로 변해가고 있다.

이러한 제 문제를 해결하기 위하여, 오늘날 우리 앞에는 다음과 같은 중대한 3대 과제가 있다.

첫째, 인간과 자연의 화해
둘째, 종교 간의 화해
셋째, 지식과 삶의 화해

이 3대 과제는 이미 우주 삼천대천세계[4]의 청정법신이신 비로자나 부처님의 청정무구한 진리로 이미 모두 해결 방안이 마련되어 있다.

사바세계를 함께 살아가는 생의 도반들이여! 오욕[5]과 칠정[6]으로 두 눈이 어두운 중생衆生과 지나친 알음알이로 하심下心을 하지 못하는 무지한 지식인들을 위하

---

4 **3천대천세계三千大天世界** 세계를 천 개 합한 것을 소천세계라 하고, 소천세계를 천 개 합한 것으로 중천세계, 중천세계를 천 개 합한 것을 대천세계라 한다. 이 대천세계를 3천대천세계라 한다.

5 **오욕五慾**은 진성眞性을 더럽히는 색色·성聲·향香·미味·촉觸의 다섯 가지 경계五境에 대해서 일어나게 되는 욕정, 즉 안眼·이耳·비鼻·설舌·신身의 다섯 가지 티끌(五塵)에서 생기는 욕망을 칭하여, 색욕·재욕·음식욕·명예욕·수면욕을 오욕五慾이라 한다.

6 **칠정七情**은 인간이 갖고 있는 기쁨喜·성냄怒·슬픔(哀)·즐거움(樂)·사랑(愛)·미움(惡)·욕망(欲)의 일곱 가지 감정을 말한다.

여, 우리 다함께 중생계衆生界와 허공계[7]가 다할 때까지 위없는 법음[8]을 듣고 싶지 않은가!

비로자나불! 부처님의 무구한 진리 자체가 법신임을 확신하게 하며 소우주의 위대한 즉신성불[9]임이 분명하다. 비로자나 부처님은 숲에서 나무를 찾고 바다에서 물을 찾는 중생들에게 마치 사바세계에 떠오르는 태양과 어두운 밤에 밝은 보름달과 같이 언제 어디서나 비추지 아니함이 없다.

현재를 살아가는 모든 세상 사람들은 물론, 흙 한 줌·풀 한 포기·나무 한 그루·벌레 한 마리 등과 같은 일체만물一切萬物이 모두 법신체[10]이며, 나의 생명과 다를 바

---

7 허공계虛空界는 진여를 말하며, 빛도 없고, 모양도 없으면서 일체 만유를 온통 휩싸고 있는 것이 허공과 같으므로 이렇게 이름한다.
8 법음法音은 법의 소리를 말한다. 법음이 털구멍에 들어가 '보리菩提의 인因'이 된다는 말로 '법음모공法音毛孔'이라 한다.
9 즉신성불卽身成佛은 밀교의 성불관으로 오랜 수행 과정을 거쳐 부처가 되는 것이 아니라, 이 몸 그대로 부처가 되는 성불을 의미한다.

없으니 다함께 성불하도록 대자비를 베푸소서!

나무[11]암밤람함캄[12] 청정법신 대교주[13]
비로자나 부처님!

종일[14] 합장合掌

10 법신체法身體는 부처의 고유한 본성으로 모든 중생을 깨우치는 고유하며 소멸되지 않는 광명을 갖고 있는 부처님의 몸인 법신을 의미한다.

11 나무南無는 산스크리트어 namas의 음역으로, 목숨을 다 바쳐 돌아가 의지한다는 뜻이며 자신의 모든 것을 던져 자기 자신을 생각하지 않는 마음이 곧 나무이다.

12 암밤람함캄暗鍐喃含坎은 우주 청정법계에 상주하고 법의 바다(法海)인 반야般若를 통하여 말로서 표현할 수 없을 만큼 분별을 여읜 큰 가르침을 주시는 비로자나 부처님을 나타내는 진언(眞言: mantra)이다.

13 대교주大敎主는 교설敎說과 교화敎化를 베푸는 교주를 말하며, 화엄종華嚴宗에서는 비로자나불毘盧遮那佛, 밀교密敎에서는 대일여래大日如來, 천태종에서는 보신報身, 『법화경』에서는 응신應身을 교주로 한다. 일반적으로 불교는 석존釋尊의 교법敎法이므로 석존을 교주라 하고, 대은교주大恩敎主라고 하지만, 후세 종파에 따라서 불신佛身에 관한 견해가 달라짐에 따라 교주의 신격身格에 대해서도 여러 가지 설이 생기게 되었다.

14 종일(宗一: 1951~현재)은 보경사(普鏡寺: 경기 성남시 중원구 하대원동 115-16번지)의 주지이며, 덕오당 법성의 제자이다.

호수의 연꽃 어느 곳에 있어도 물들지 않는 청정한 꽃(처렴상정處染常淨)

비밀교秘密敎 오방관五方觀

암暗	금강부 金剛部	동방 東方	아촉불 阿閦佛	대원경지 大圓鏡智	아뢰야식 阿賴耶識	간肝
밤鑁	연화부 蓮華部	서방 西方	아미타불 阿彌陀佛	묘관찰지 妙觀察智	제육의식 第六意識	폐肺
람覽	보생부 寶生部	남방 南方	보생불 寶生佛	평등성지 平等性智	제칠식 第七識	심心
함含	갈마부 羯摩部	북방 北方	불공성취불 不空成就佛	성소작지 成所作智	제오식 第五識	신腎
캄坎	불부 佛部	중앙 中央	대일여래 大日如來	법계체성지 法界體性智	여래장식 如來藏識	비脾
오주 五呪	오부 五部	오방 五方	오불 五佛	오지 五智	오식 五識	오장 五臟

서문

나는 어려서 원인 모를 병으로 백약이 무효하여 스물두 살에 관세음보살觀世音菩薩님전에 귀의하여 지극정성으로 기도하던 중, 관세음보살님의 계시啓示를 받고, 무술(1958)년 10월 부산에서 경남 창녕군 영축산靈鷲山으로 입산入山했다.

일을 기도 삼고 기도를 일 삼아 주야 일심으로 기도하니 영축산에 간 지 한 달도 채 못 되어 관세음보살님의 자비은덕慈悲恩德으로 20여 년 동안 고통 받던 병고에서 벗어났다. 그때부터 나는 부처님 은혜에 보답하고자 불당[15]을 이룩하여 사회의 병든 중생을 구제공덕하

---

15 **불당佛堂**은 불·보살의 상을 안치한 전당으로, 우리나라에서는 흔히 법당이라 한다.

려는 원을 세워 부처님전에 "이 한 몸 고통 받아 누만 중생에게 도움이 된다면 고생을 복으로 삼고 노력하겠습니다."라고 서원[16]하고 여러 절간으로 다니면서 불철주야 일념정진[17] 기도했다.

갑진년(1964) 10월 경남 창녕군 영축산 대인골 토굴에서 청정법신 비로자나 부처님께서 주야 3개월 동안 법문하실 때 "천지우주 삼라만상 진대지가 나의 전신체이다."라고 하셨다. "너는 내 제자로서 앞으로 세계만방에 비로자나불 법을 펴는 교주가 될 것이다."라는 예언을 하셨다.

그리고 청정법신 비로자나 부처님께서 나의 이마를

---

[16] 서원誓願은 원願을 발하여 그것을 이루고자 맹세하는 것이다. 대표적인 서원은 '사홍서원四弘誓願'으로, 불교에 귀의한 모든 사람들이 세워야 하는 "중생을 다 건지리이다. 번뇌를 다 끊으리라. 법문을 다 배우리라. 불도를 다 이루리라."라는 4가지 큰 서원이다.

[17] 일념정진一念精進은 한결같은 생각, 하나의 마음으로 열심히 노력하며 악행을 버리고 선행을 닦는 것을 뜻한다.

만져 주시면서 하시는 말씀이 "법성, 너는 누만대로 나의 제자이다. 지금부터 불당을 이룩하여 나의 법을 펼치라"고 수기[18]하시고 주야 3개월 동안 법문하셨다. 그때부터 나는 지금까지 비로자나 부처님 법을 펴나오고 있다.

덕오당 법성[19] 합장

---

[18] **수기**授記는 기별記別・수기受記・기설記說・수결受決・기記라고 번역하며, 내생來生에 부처가 되겠다든가 어떻게 되리라는 것을 미리 전하거나 기록 받는 것을 뜻한다.

[19] **덕오당 법성**法性(1928~2005)은 소승(종일)의 은사로서, 법성사法性寺(경남 창녕군 계성면 사리) 주지를 역임한 바 있다.(『나의 길 50여 년』, 전게서)

毘盧遮那佛 經

南無 一心奉請 清淨光明

法身光明 諸佛通證

無量壽 毘盧遮那佛

창녕 법성사 대광명전 영축산 기슭(계성면 사리)에 덕오당 법성(1928~2005)이 대광명전(1996년 창건)에 비로자나불을 봉안하여 일생동안 비로자나불 법을 펴시었다.

제1장 비로자나불의 위신력[20]

비로자나불은 광명변조불[21] 또는 대일여래[22]라고 한다. 대일은 태양을 말한다. 태양의 광명은 비로자나불의 광명과 비슷하므로 대일여래라고 한다. 태양은 제암변명[23] 능성중무[24] 광무생멸[25]의 세 가지 큰 속성을

---

20 위신력은 불과위佛果位에 있는 존엄尊嚴하고 헤아릴 수 없는 불가사의不可思議한 힘을 말한다.
21 광명변조불光明遍照佛은 모든 중생을 무한한 공덕의 빛인 광명변조로 구해주시는 부처님을 뜻한다.
22 대일여래大日如來는 산스크리트어 Mahavairocana의 의역으로, 밀교의 본존이다. '마하摩訶'는 크다(大), '비로자나'라는 일日이라는 뜻이어서 대일大日이라고 한다.
23 제암변명除暗遍明은 비로자나 부처님의 보편적인 성격을 나타내는 것이다.

가지고 있다. 태양은 어둠 속에 빛을 비추어서 두루 밝게 하고, 초목총림을 비롯한 삼라만상들은 그 햇빛을 받아 그들의 성품에 따라 자란다. 그러나 태양의 광명은 광대한 공덕은 있어도 제한이 있어, 낮에만 비추고 밤에는 비추지 않고, 밖에 비치면 안에는 비치지 못하고, 운무에 가리면 빛이 보이지 않으며, 깊은 굴속이나 물속에 그 빛이 미치지 못하고, 밝음이 한쪽에 있으면 다른 쪽에는 이르지 못한다.

그렇지만, 비로자나 부처님의 광명은 제한이 없다.

부처님의 지혜는 모든 것을 두루 밝게 하여 그림자를 드리울 곳도 없고 낮과 밤 구별도 없기 때문에 세간의 태양보다 더 큰 태양(大日)을 의미한다.

24 능성중무能成衆務는 비로자나 부처님의 중생에 대한 자비활동을 설하는 것이다. 태양은 생물을 성장시키는 근원이 되지만, 부처님의 빛은 두루 퍼지면서 모든 생명이 지닌 특성을 발휘시키고 일체작물을 완성시킨다.

25 광무생멸光無生滅은 비로자나 부처님이 나타난 진리의 영원불멸성을 표현한 것이다. 구름이 있고 없음에 관계없이 태양은 존재하고, 그 빛은 나거나 멸하는 일 없이 세계를 끊임없이 비추는 것과 같이, 대일여래인 비로자나 부처님은 중생을 위하여 항상 법을 설하고 있다.

제1장 비로자나불의 위신력 **27**

홍련암 일출 천지에 빛을 밝혀 어둠을 몰아내고 만물을 소생시키는 대일여래 (大日如來: 太陽)

낮과 밤, 안과 밖의 구별 없이 무한하고 무차별하여 일체 도처에 두루하지 않는 곳이 없다. 중생의 내면에 있는 무명번뇌의 암운까지도 덜고, 두루 밝게 비추고, 세간의 여러 일들이 비로자나 부처님의 위신력으로 이루어지지 않는 것이 없는 불생불멸한 부처님이므로 광명변조인 즉 생불이시다.

비로자나 부처님은 법신불[26]이요, 이치의 불이며 근본불이시다. 법신불이란 진리 자체를 말한다. 그러므로 시작도 끝도 없으며 영구 불멸한 부처님이시기 때문에, 법신불은 어떠한 형상을 나타낼 수가 없지만, 8세기에 지권인[27]으로 맺은 불상으로 형상화되어 예배의 대상이 되었다. 동양문화권에서 무수히 나타났던 부처님들은 비록 비로자나라는 명호名號를 띠지 않았더라도 모두 비로자나불, 즉 진리와 법法으로 형상화하였던 것이다.

비로자나불은 자성[28]이며 심이며 불이며 본체이며 만유[29]이며 삼라만상森羅萬象이며 법계[30]이다. 그러므로

---

26 법신불法身佛은 우주만유의 본원本願과 제불제성의 심인心印, 그리고 일체중생의 본성本性을 말하며, 사은의 본성과 여래의 불성을 법신불이라 하고, 청정법신불이라 명명하기도 하며 응화불〔應化佛: 각주 64〕로 칭하기도 한다.

27 지권인智拳印은 대일여래의 수인으로, 제불의 지혜의 법해法海를 집지한 표상이다. 부처님과 중생은 같은 것이며, 미혹함과 깨달음도 본래는 하나라는 뜻을 나타낸 것이라고 한다.

28 자성自性은 모든 살아 있는 유정체의 본유의 성질을 뜻하며, 자성본불自性本佛이라 하면 본래부터 갖추어 있는 고유한 불성佛性을 말한다.

축서사 석조비로자나불상 9세기경 통일신라시대 좌불상으로 경북 봉화 축서사 보광전에 봉안되어 있다(보물 제995호).

일즉다·다즉일[31]의 원리가 실현된다. 천지우주 삼라

---

29 만유萬有는 불교에서 오온五蘊·십이처十二處·십팔계十八界, 즉 존재하는 모든 것을 의미한다. 이 중 오온은 존재의 다섯 가지 측면을 나타내고 있고, 12처와 18계는 무명촉으로 점철된 주관적인 인식을 중심으로 전개되는 존재의 현주소를 나타내고 있다.

30 법계法界는 부처의 18계의 하나로서, 의식意識의 대상인 모든 사물을 말한다.

31 일즉다一卽多·다즉일多卽一은 하나(一) 속에 많은(多) 것이 포함되어 있고

만상이 비로자나불의 현현[32]이라면 무엇이든지 비로자나불 아님이 없다. 그러므로 근원적이고 보편적인 진리인 청정법신 비로자나불은 진리 그 자체이므로 모든 종파宗派를 초월한다. 우주가 진리이며 생생요요하게 현전하는 우주의 진리 그 자체를 법신이라 한다.

법신은 만유본체의 진리로 모든 부처님의 진신이다. 우주만유에 상주불멸[33]하는 진여인 법신은 어떠한 개념이나 물체가 아니라 그것은 증득[34]되어져야 하는 것이며, 증득은 수행을 통해서만 나타나는 것이다. 말하자면 정각[35]을 이루어서 무명[36]을 멸하고 지혜를

많은(多) 것 속에 하나(一)의 속성이 포함되어 있다는 뜻이다.

32 현현顯現은 명백하게 나타나거나 나타내는 것을 의미한다.
33 상주불멸常住不滅은 본연진심本然眞心이 없어지지 아니하고 영원히 존재함을 의미하며, 상주부단常住不斷과 같은 뜻이다.
34 증득證得은 깨달음 차원을 넘어서 '일체경계를 뛰어넘어 마음의 지혜를 성취한 경지'이다. 궁극의 깨달음인 일심증득一心證得은 의식적인 신해행신信解行의 차원을 뛰어 넘어야 한다.
35 정각正覺은 깨달음, 또는 부처로 되는(깨닫는) 순간을 뜻한다. 부처님의

얻음으로써 법신을 알 수 있다. 정각正覺하면 사바세계 그대로가 극락정토極樂淨土와 청정법계로 변하기 때문이다.

극락은 서방정토西方淨土에만 있는 것이 아니라 자기 안의 자성에 있으며, 다른 이가 구해주는 것이 아니라 자기 자신의 힘으로 실현하는 것이다. 모든 것이 정각에 수렴되듯이 모든 불보살은 비로자나불을 중심으로 상즉[37]이 된다. 그러함으로써 비로자나불의 세계가 바로 연화장장엄세계[38]가 되는 것이다.

깨달음은 위없고 비길 데 없는 가장 올바른 깨달음으로, 산스크리트어 '아뇩다라삼먁삼보리(Anuttara-Samyak-Sambodhi)'를 의역하여 무상정등각無上正等覺이라 한다.

36 **무명無明**은 진리에 눈뜨지 못하고 사물에 통달하지 못해서 사물과 현상의 도리를 확실하게 이해할 수 없는 정신상태이며 어리석음이다. 사물의 있는 그대로의 모습을 보지 못하는 불여실지견不如實智見을 말한다.

37 **상즉相卽**은 두 개의 사상思象이 서로를 버리고 무차별無差別의 하나가 되는 것을 말한다.

38 **연화장장엄세계蓮華藏莊嚴世界**는 화엄경에서 일컫는 연화의 세계로, 연화장세계 또는 화장세계라고도 한다.

불국사 금동비로자나불상 통일신라시대 3대 불상으로 꼽히며 비로전에 봉안되어 있다(국보 제26호).

연화장장엄세계는 곧 불국토이다. 비로자나 부처님은 삼세에 항상 변함없이 설법하는 부처님이며, 온 우주에 두루 미치고 법계원만한 절대신이다. 모든 제불보살은 이 법신불의 가지신[39]으로 나타나며, 방편

---

39 **가지신**加持身은 중생을 가지加持하는 불佛이 방편으로 중생의 근기에 알맞은 몸을 나타내어 설법·교화하는 불신佛身이다. 응신應身, 또는 응화신應化身이라고도 한다.

으로써 중생에게 생명을 주고 진리를 설하고 있다. 그러므로 비로자나 부처님은 일체제불의 총본불인 생불이시다.

청정법신 비로자나 부처님은 연화장극락세계에 계시옵고 그 원력이 광대무변廣大無邊하시고, 몸과 마음이 맑고 깨끗한 금색광명이 온 허공에 가득 차고 그 위엄과 세력이 전지전능하시다. 천지우주 삼라만상 법계에 참된 광명을 두루 비추어 만물을 소생케 하시고 모든 중생의 병고액난을 구제하시고 죄악을 소멸하시며, 각자의 원을 성취시켜 주신다. 그래서 비로자나 부처님은 곧 일월과 같으시다.

세계만방에 자연적으로 미묘한 형태가 각각으로 원만하게 되어 있는 그 상호를 낱낱이 드러내 보여주시는 그것이 곧 비로자나 부처님의 위신력이며 생불의 광명조화이다.

동굴 속 빛 동굴 속의 빛도 비로자나불의 위신력이며 광명조화 (승솟동굴: Surprise Cave 베트남 하롱베이)

제2장 비로자나불 십신불[40]

1. 중앙 화장세계華藏世界에서 형상形相을 저 진법계[41]에 두루 널리 펼치시는 청정한 허공신 비로자나불
2. 위엄 있는 광명 빛나 비추는 것 그만두게 할 수 없는 그 위세 대단히 뛰어난 몸 비로자나불
3. 끝없이 오묘한 색신[42] 청정한 복덕福德을 구족한 매우 광대한 몸 비로자나불

---

40 십신불十身佛은 부처님이 열 가지 몸을 다 갖추고 있다는 뜻이다.
41 진법계眞法界는 부처님의 진실세계를 뜻하며, 이 세계는 다시 거짓과 참의 세계로 구분된다.
42 색신色身은 부처님이나 보살의 육신肉身, 색상이 있는 몸, 맨눈으로 보이는 형체, 곧 육체를 칭한다.

4. 일체 부처님의 국토에서 모두 다 뜻에 따라 몸을 받아 나툰 비로자나불

5. 티끌수와 같은 상호와 둥글고 밝으며 원만구족[43]한 상호로 장엄한 몸 비로자나불

6. 감응感應에 따라 빈틈없이 산하에 나투어 큰 원력[44]으로 법을 설하시는 몸 비로자나불

7. 갖가지 화신불[45] 몸을 따라 나온 자재[46]한 응화신[47]

---

[43] 원만구족圓滿具足은 부처님의 삶과 같은 깨달음의 경지인 진리를 표현하는 말이다. 모자라거나 부족함이 없이 모든 것을 두루 갖추어 있다는 뜻으로서, 곧 일원상의 진리를 나타낸다. 원만구족한 일원상의 진리 일체를 받아 일상생활에 그대로 활용하는 불·보살의 인격과 일원의 위력을 얻고 일원의 체성에 합한 경지를 의미한다.

[44] 원력願力은 원하는 바를 이루려는 간절한 마음의 힘, 즉 서원誓願·소원의 힘이라는 뜻으로, 본원력·숙원력·대업원력이라고도 한다.

[45] 화신불化身佛은 부처님의 3신身 중 하나로서, 화신불은 응신불應身佛·응화신應化身·변화신變化身이라고도 한다. 화신불은 중생들의 간절한 염원에 따라 그를 제도하고자 나타내시는 부처님을 말한다.

[46] 자재自在는 마음대로 무엇이나 자유롭지 않은 것이 없고 모든 것에 걸림 없음을 일컫는 말로서, 불·보살이 갖추고 있는 공덕 중 하나이다.

[47] 응화신應化身은 부처님의 삼신三身 중 하나로 중생을 교화하기 위해 여러 가지 형상으로 변화하여 나타나는 것을 말한다. 석가모니 부처님이 대표적이다.

비로자나불

8. 지혜의 광명 밝고 밝아 널리 세간에 비추어 현상에 섭입[48]된 오묘한 지혜의 몸 비로자나불

9. 낱낱의 도량道場에 몸과 지혜가 모두 노니는 크나큰 한 줄의 정법신[49] 비로자나불

10. 본래의 자리를 떠나지 않고도 널리 신비한 힘을 펼치는 의보정보[50]의 몸을 가진 비로자나불

온갖 장애障碍가 다하고 갖가지 덕상[51] 원만하며 광대한 생각을 내어 광명을 널리 비추는 국토國土·중생·업보신[52]으로, 성문[53]·연각[54]·보살신[55]으로, 여래의 지

---

48 섭입攝入은 부처님이 나에게 들어오고 나 역시 부처님께 들어가는 입아아입入我我入의 뜻을 가지라 하는 것이다.

49 정법신正法身은 보살신으로, 정법을 말하여 중생을 교화하고 이익이 있게 한다.

50 의보정보依報正報에서 과거 업업의 갚음으로 얻은 유정有情의 몸을 정보正報라 하고, 그 몸이 의지하고 있는 환경, 곧 국토인 기세간器世間을 의보依報라 한다

51 덕상德相은 부처님의 수승한 상호相好를 말하는 것이다.

52 업보신業報身은 전세의 악업에 의해 받은 몸 그대로가 불신佛身이라는

혜 몸과 법신으로, 허공과 같이 두루 보편한 허공신虛
空身으로 이와 같이 내외內外로 열 가지 몸을 갖추신
비로자나불이다.

해인사 대적광전 해인사 대적광전에 주불인 비로자나불이 봉안
되어 있다(3보 사찰 중 법보사찰).

뜻이다. 해경십불解境十佛의 하나이다. 해경십불은 깨달음의 경계에
있는 열 가지 불신佛身을 말하는데, 국토신, 중생신, 업보신,성문신,
연각신, 보살신, 여래신, 지신, 법신, 허공신이다.

53 **성문**聲聞은 부처님의 말씀을 듣고 깨닫는 자를 뜻하며, 부처님의 제자를
일컫는다.

54 **연각**緣覺은 홀로 깨닫는 사람을 말한다. 남의 말에 의하지 않고 스스로
무상함을 깨달아서, 인연이 흩어짐을 따라 진여를 체달하나니 이를
연각이라 한다.

55 **보살신**菩薩身은 보살의 몸이 그대로 부처(佛身)라는 뜻이다. 해경십불의
하나이다.

제3장 법신불

비로자나 부처님은 법신불을 말함이요, 석가모니 부처님은 화신불을 말함이다. 석가불이 깨친 법은 과거 불도 깨친지라, 법이라고 하는 것은 일체세간[56] 그 현상을 곧 그대로 보는 고로 세간 본래 법칙이라. 그것은 곧 석가불이 출세하지 않더라도 과거 모든 부처님이 각[57]을 하지 않더라도 일정하게 있으므로

---

56 일체세간一切世間은 모든 유정有情 중생이 서로 의지하며 살아가는 세상을 말한다.
57 각覺은 깨달음을 뜻하며, 혹은 '깨달은 자'를 뜻하여 부처님을 가리키기도 한다.

변함없는 것이니라.

이와 같은 불변법[58]이 불의 본체[59] 되는 고로 불은 법과 일치하여 각보다는 체득[60]이니 이는 오직 자신이 곧 법이 됨을 이름이라. 법은 원래 시종始終없고 영구 불변함으로써 일관하게 있으므로 이것이 곧 참 부처며, 세간 모든 사람들이 진실도를 모르고서 고통하고 있는 것을 애민哀愍하게 생각하여 중생들을 제도코자 출세하신 이 부처를 석가라고 이름이니, 이와 같은 진리에서 법신부처 이외에는 다른 부처 없으므로 석가불이 출세함은 법신불의 방편[61]으로 화현[62]하신 것

---

58 **불변법不變法**은 고쳐지지도 변화하지 않는 법이다. 불교에서는 이 세상이 가고 다음 세상이 오고, 다음다음 생이 와도 변하지 않는 법칙, 그것을 진리라고 하고, 그것을 안 사람이 깨달은 사람, 곧 '부처님'이라고 한다.
59 **본체本體**는 모든 사상의 근본을 이루는 체體, 제법의 근본 자체, 진신眞身 등을 의미한다.
60 **체득體得**은 인간이 자신의 몸으로 체험하여 얻어지는 부처님의 진리를 의미한다.
61 **방편方便**의 방方은 방법, 편便은 편리이니, 일체 중생의 근기에 계합하는 방법과 수단을 편리하게 쓰는 것을 의미한다.

이니라.

해인사 대비로전 이 건물은 화재 및 지진에 대비해 열 감지기와 진동 측정기 등 첨단장비가 설치된 200㎡ 규모의 전각으로, 화재 또는 지진이 나면 불상이 지하 6m 별실로 자동 이동시켜져 안전하게 보호된다. 2005년 5월 개금을 위해 복장유물을 개봉하다가 발견된 '묵서명墨書銘'에 의해 현존 최고最古 목조불상인 쌍비로자나불상(883년)으로 밝혀졌다.

62 **화현化現**은 부처님이나 보살이 중생을 교화하고 구제하기 위한 수단으로 여러 가지 모습으로 변하여 세상사에 나투시는 것을 의미한다.

제4장 보신불

원願을 세워 수행하여 그 과보로 부처되니 석가여래釋迦如來 이전에도 많은 부처 있는지라. 아미타불阿彌陀佛 다보여래多寶如來 약사여래藥師如來 모든 부처 중생 위해 원을 세워 보신부처[63] 되시니라.

---

63 **보신부처報身佛陀**는 무량광이라는 빛으로 이루어져 있으며, 영원히 손상되지 않고 오염되지 않으며, 32상 80종호 이상으로 희유하고 거룩한 몸이다. 우주적인 능력을 갖추고 있으며 지혜와 자비, 그리고 진리 그 자체이다.

제5장 응화불[64]

비로자나 부처님을 법신이라 하였으며 석가모니 부처님을 응신이라 하였으니 법신불을 알려 하면 먼저 삼신[65] 알지니라. 석가모니 부처님이 출가고행出家苦行하신 것은 시현示現으로 중생들에 도 닦는 법 가르치고 생로병사 모든 고통 여의는 법 보였으며, 사라쌍수[66] 숲속에서 열반상涅槃相을 나타냄은 중생들에 무

---

64 응화불應化佛은 응신應身·화신化身이라고도 한다. 중생을 구제하기 위하여 여러 가지 몸으로 나타낸 부처님을 뜻한다.
65 삼신三身은 불신佛身을 그 특성에 따라 셋으로 나눈 것으로 법신法身·보신報身·응신應身을 말한다.
66 사라쌍수沙羅雙樹는 석가모니 부처님께서 열반涅槃에 드신 핍팔라 나무숲

상[67]함을 알려주기 위하여서 일시 모양 감췄으나 진신만은 부동이니, 세간[68] 모든 현상 응하여 나타난 몸 응신[69]이라.

운주사 탑 전남 화순 운주사 법당까지 이르는 길에 있는 다수의 탑들은 청정법신과 함께하는 불법 인연.

을 말한다.
67 무상無常은 모든 존재는 변화하며, 고정불변하거나 영원한 것은 없음을 뜻한다.
68 세간世間은 현상 세계, 혹은 존재의 모든 현상을 이르는 말이다.
69 응신應身은 법·보·응 3신三身 중 하나로, 중생을 교화하려는 부처님이 중생과 같은 몸을 나타내신 것이다.

제6장 법신불의 본유[70]

법신불은 본래 있어 보리심[71]에 비유하고 화신불은 닦아나니 보리행菩提行에 비유한다.
법신불이 중생 위해 당신이 곧 화신되니 법신부처 이밖에는 다시 부처 없는지라.

---

70 **본유本有**는 본래 갖추고 있음을 뜻하며, 어떠한 수행을 하지 않고도 선천적으로 구유하고 있는 덕성을 뜻한다. 원래부터 갖추어져 있어 성性이란 말로 표현할 때도 있다.

71 **보리심菩提心**은 분별을 여의고 지혜로 깨달은 마음을 뜻한다. 모든 중생들은 자기 마음에 밝은 등불의 지혜가 있음을 알지 못하고 있을 뿐, 이것을 자각自覺하여 어둠의 장벽을 깨뜨릴 때 비로소 자연히 모든 괴로움의 묶임에서 자유로워질 수 있다는 것이다.

법신불은 태양같고 화신불은 만월滿月같다. 그러므로 법신명호法身名號 비로자나 대일이라.

밀교[72]본신 양陽인 고로 현세정화 위주하며 밀교본신 양을 쓰고 현세안락現世安樂 서원하여 이 땅 정토淨土 만듦으로 진호국가[73] 서원하여 자기성불自己成佛 하기 위해 식재[74]하고 증익[75]하고 항복降伏받고 경애敬愛되니 국민 모두 안락하고 국토 모두 성불된다. 이것이 곧 오는 세상 몇 천 겁[76]을 기다려서 성불함이 아니므로

---

72 밀교密敎는 비밀의 가르침이란 뜻으로, 문자 언어로 표현된 현교顯敎를 초월한 최고심원最高深遠한 가르침을 말한다. 금강승金剛乘이라고도 한다.

73 진호국가鎭護國家는 부처님의 진리로 국가를 수호한다는 뜻이다. 국난을 멈추게 하고 국가를 태평하게 하기 위하여 진리를 닦는 것(修法)을 말한다. 『인왕반야경仁王般若經』이나 『금강명경金剛明經』에 의하면 국왕이나 국민이 이 경을 수지하고 독송하면, 7난七難을 소멸하며 국가를 진호鎭護한다고 한다.

74 식재息災는 4종단법의 하나로, 밀교에서 온갖 재해와 고난을 없애는 법이다. 4종단법은 식재·증익·항복·경애이다.

75 증익增益은 4종단법의 하나로, 행복과 덕을 얻는 수행 방법 중 하나이다.

76 겁劫은 하늘과 땅이 한 번 개벽開闢할 때부터 다음 개벽할 때까지의 동안이라는 뜻으로서, 지극히 길고 오랜 시간을 이르는 말이다.

즉신성불이라 한다.

수인사 금동비로자나불상 경남 김해 아우산에 위치한 수인사 대적광전에는 금동비로자나불 좌상과 입상 2존 불상이 모셔져 있다.

제7장 진언밀교 불신관

진언밀교眞言密敎 불신관은 석가불이 출세함은 비로자나 법신불이 세간 사람 애민하여 가작[77]으로 정반왕의 태자로서 출생하고 출가하여 고행 닦아 성불하는 그 모양을 일체 모든 중생들에 보여주신 것으로서, 현교[78] 불신관과 같이 응신에서 소급하여 그로부터

---

77 가작假作은 법신불인 비로자나 부처님이 우주의 진리를 사바세계 중생들에게 깨우치고자 화신불이 되기 위하여, 정반왕과 마야부인 사이에 싣달타(Siddhattha Gotama)태자로 태어남을 일컫는다.

78 현교顯敎는 밀교密敎에 대비되는데, 언어 문자상으로 분명히 설시說示된 가르침이라는 뜻으로, 밀교 이외의 불교를 가리켜 말한다.

보신법신 알게 됨이 아니니라.

법신불이 먼저 있어 그로부터 응신불應身佛 나고 보신불도 나타나니 진언밀교 삼신[79]관은 사신관[80]이 되는 고로 현밀불신 상대하면 밀교사종 법신이요 현교삼신 법보응화應化[81]라.

자성신[82]은 법신이요 수용신[83]은 보신이요 변화신[84]은 응신이요 등류신[85]도 응신이며 화신이고 응화신이라.

---

[79] 삼신관三身觀은 부처님은 법신法身·보신報身·응신應身 또는 화신化身의 3가지 몸을 가지고 있다는 사상 또는 교의이다.

[80] 사신관四身觀은 불신佛身을 법신·보신·응신·화신의 4종으로 바라보는 견해이다. 법신은 진여의 이체理體, 보신은 수행이 완성되어 복과 지혜가 원만한 것, 응신은 석존과 같이 기류機類에 맞추어 나타난 것, 화신은 응신에서 일시 변화하는 것을 의미한다.

[81] 응화는 부처님의 삼신三身 가운데 응신應身·화신化身·응화신應化身을 말한다.

[82] 자성신自性身은 밀교에서 세운 4신四身 가운데, 일체법의 본체이며 제불의 본불本佛인 대일여래를 말한다.

[83] 수용신受用身은 법·보·응 3신三身 가운데 보신報身과 같다. 깨달음의 결과로 얻은 법락을 자신만 즐기려는 자수용신, 타인에게도 느끼게 하려는 타수용신이 있다.

[84] 변화신變化身은 법·보·응 3신의 하나로서, 2승乘과 범부를 교화하기 위하여 성소작지成所作智의 힘에 의하여 화현한 불신을 의미한다.

우포늪 해돋이 70여 만 평에 이르며 1억 4천만 년 전의 원시적 저층 늪이 천연 그대로 간직되어 있다. 350여 종의 희귀 동식물이 대일여래의 빛 해돋이를 매일 맞이하여 그들의 낙원을 만든 더할 나위 없는 아름다운 습지이다(1999년 자연습지지정).

---

85 등류신等流身은 4종四種 법신法身의 하나로, 부처님의 몸이 변화하여 사람·하늘·귀신·짐승과 같은 모양을 나타내는 것을 말한다.

제8장 법신불의 체상용

법신불의 체상용[86]은 육대六大 사만[87] 삼밀[88]로서 모든 사실 설법이요 활동하는 경전經典이라. 생명 없는 그 진리는 인과因果로써 나타나니 사지 사력[89] 활동으

---

86 **체상용**體相用은 『기신론』에서 설한 3대를 말한다. 진여를 체體, 지혜·자비 등의 무량공덕을 상相, 이체와 상이 연에 응해서 활동하는 것을 용用이라 한다.
87 **사만**四曼은 네 가지 만다라, 즉 대만다라大曼茶羅, 삼매야만다라三昧耶曼茶羅, 법만다라法曼茶羅, 갈마만다라(karma-曼茶羅)이다.
88 **삼밀**三密은 밀교 수행법의 하나로, 신밀身密, 구밀口密, 의밀意密을 말한다.
89 **사지**四智 사력四力에서 사지는 부처님이 지닌 4가지 지혜로, 대원경지大圓鏡智, 평등성지平等性智, 묘관찰지妙觀察智, 성소작지成所作智를 말하고, 사력은 신력信力, 정진력精進力, 정력定力, 혜력慧力을 말한다.

로 생활 중에 각할지라.

일은 복지[90]전수이니 삼밀행[91]과 희사[92]로써 복덕지혜[93] 구족하게 부지런히 닦을지요, 이는 사리[94]필구이니 내가 당한 모든 일에 그 이치를 연구하고 판단하여 볼 것이요, 삼은 생활 취사取捨이니 공사생활 모든 일에 선악시비 선후본말 취사하여 행할지요, 사는 결과 내증[95]이니 자기 행한 모든 일에 공사손익 그 인과를 증득하여 볼 것이라. 이와 같이 실행하면

---

90 **복지福智**는 부처님이 되기 위해서 중생들이 체득해야 할 복과 지혜福智를 말한다.

91 **삼밀행三密行**은 신·구·의身口意의 비밀스러운 행위를 뜻한다.

92 **희사喜捨**는 기쁘게 재물을 보시하는 것을 말한다. 불성이 부처로 나타나는 것이 최고의 이상적인 인격을 이루는 것을 뜻하는 '자비희사慈悲喜捨·사무량심四無量心'이라는 글귀에서 유래된 말이다.

93 **지혜智慧**는 육바라밀의 하나로, 사물의 실상을 비추어 올바르게 진리를 인식하는 것을 말한다.

94 **사리事理**의 사事는 상대적이며 차별이 있는 현상을, 이理는 절대적이며 평등한 진리를 뜻한다.

95 **내증內證**은 자내증自內證이라고도 한다. 마음속으로 진리를 증득하는 것으로 자기 마음(自己心) 안의 깨달음을 뜻하며, 본질의 깨달음을 성취하는 경지인 아뇩다라삼먁삼보리를 얻은 것이다.

모든 서원 만족하여 복지구족[96] 하게 되며 현세정화 되느니라.

만다라의 만덕장엄

96 **복지구족福智具足**은 보살이 부처가 되기 위해서 지혜를 닦아 자신의 깨달음을 완성하기 위한 지행智行·지업智業과 갖가지 선행으로 다른 사람에게 자비를 베풀어 자신의 덕을 쌓는 복행福行·복업福業의 두 가지가 경건해야 한다.

제9장 당체법문[97]

시방삼세[98] 나타나는 일체 모든 사실들과 내가 체험하고 있는 좋고 나쁜 모든 일은 법신불의 당체로서 활동하는 설법이라. 밀은 색[99]으로 하여 일체세간 현상대

---

97 당체법문當體法門에서 당체는 본체, 즉 변치 않는 진리로서 법신불을 나타내며, 법문은 지혜의 문을 말한다.

98 시방삼세十方三世에서 시방은 동·서·남·북 사방과 동남·동북·서남·서북의 사유에다 상·하를 합하여 열 가지의 방향을 나타낸 말이며, 삼세는 과거세·현재세·미래세를 이르는 말이다. 불교에서 시방은 공간적인 개념을 나타낸 말이고, 삼세는 시간적인 개념을 나타낸 말이다.

99 밀密은 색色에서 색色은 감각적이고 물질적인 것으로 눈으로 보이는 모든 것, 즉 사람과 살아 있는 모든 것, 자연과 자연현상 및 태양·별·우주, 모두가 색이다. 그리고 밀密한 것은 공空이며, 색 뒤에 숨어 있는 힘이고

로 불의 법과 일치하게 체득함이 교리이니, 체험이 곧 법문이요 사실이 곧 경전이라. 현교경은 문자로서 유식해야 알게 되고 밀교경은 삼밀로서 무식해도 알게 된다. 오직 삼밀행자만이 이 법문을 보는 고로 유식무식 차별 없이 각각 자기 환경 따라 좋은 길과 나쁜 길을 능히 분별하게 되니 좋은 길을 버리고서 나쁜 길을 누가 가랴. 선악인과善惡因果 밝게 아니 고苦 여의고 낙樂 얻으며, 무진법문[100] 넓게 아니 깨쳐 성불하게 된다.

보이지 않는 차원의 작용으로, 보이지는 않지만 존재를 초월하여 존재하는 것이다.
100 **무진법문無盡法門**은 다하여 그치는 데가 없는 법문, 즉 무량한 법문을 말한다.

제10장 육대무애[101]

육대는 곧 지수화풍공과 식이 그 육대이니, 앞의 오대 물성[102]되고 최후 식대[103] 정신精神이라. 이 육대의 연기[104]로서 우주본체 이뤘으며 불교 원래 인간으로 근본

---

101 육대무애六大無碍는 제법의 근본요소인 지地·수水·화火·풍風·공空·식識 6대가 서로 융통하고, 섭입攝入하여 장애되지 아니함을 뜻한다.
102 물성物性은 물질이 가지고 있는 성질, 즉 물건의 보편적인 성질을 뜻한다.
103 식대識大는 6대 중 하나로, 밀교에서는 우주와 모든 존재를 구성하는 본체를 육대라 한다. 앞의 오대는 물질·자연계이고, 식대는 정신·의식계이다.
104 연기緣起는 원시 경전에 나타난 연기설의 원초적 형태는 "이것이 있으므로 저것이 있고, 이것이 생기므로 저것이 생긴다. 이것이 없으면 저것이 없고, 이것이 멸하면 저것이 멸한다."는 것이다.

삼는 교이므로 이와 같은 연기설緣起說도 그 중심은 인간이니 사람들은 누구라도 육대로써 된 것이라. 땅은 본래 견성[105]이라 일정 형용 지대[106]이요, 물은 원래 습기이므로 액체 습기 수대[107]되고, 불의 성은 더우므로 따뜻한 것 화대[108]되며, 바람 원래 동성[109]이

---

[105] 견성堅性은 사대四大 중 지地의 성질인 단단한 성질을 뜻한다. 지地는 견성堅性, 수水는 습성濕性, 화火는 난성煖性, 풍風은 동성動性의 성질을 가지고 여러 인연을 만나 취집聚集하고 조합하여 각각의 개체를 형성한다.

[106] 지대地大는 사대 중 하나로 흙의 성질을 뜻한다. 본질이 단단한 성질로서, 보호하고 간직하는(保持) 작용이 있는 것을 말한다. 지대는 만물의 첫 번째 원소이며, 모든 존재가 기대고 바탕으로 삼아 사는 곳이다.

[107] 수대水大는 사대 중 하나로 물의 성질을 뜻한다. 본질이 축축한 성질로서, 거두고 모으는 작용이 있는 것을 말한다. 수대는 감정의 자리이며 항상 수평을 유지하려 노력하고, 마음에 들면 잡아당기는 탐심貪心, 마음에 들지 않으면 미워하는 진심嗔心이 항상 자신의 위치와 존재를 소멸되지 않게 하는 역할을 한다.

[108] 화대火大(tejo-dhātu)는 사대 중 하나로 불의 성질을 뜻한다. 본질이 따뜻한 성질로서, 성숙시키는 작용이 있는 것을 말한다. 화대火大는 자성磁性의 자리이고, 에고Ego이다. 부족할 때 빨아들이고 넘치면 뱉어낸다. 어느 한 순간 사랑에서 반드시 다음 순간에 미움을 수반한다. 인간의 혼魂이 존재하는 자리에 화대火大가 있다.

[109] 동성動性은 움직임이 일어나는 것으로 풍風의 성질이다.

라 활동 변화 풍대[110]되고, 공의 성은 무애無碍이므로 사대융통[111] 공대[112]되며, 식은 아는 성이므로 심식[113]작용 식대니라. 대저 인因이 있다 해도 이를 도울 연緣 없으면 세간만물 성장하고 성공하기 어려우니, 무애연기[114] 그 원리를 진실하게 자각[115]하면 거침없는 인간

110 **풍대風大**는 사대 중 하나로 바람의 성질을 뜻한다. 본질이 움직이는 성질로서, 생장의 작용이 있는 것을 말한다. 풍대는 상념想念의 자리이다. 한 생각 지나가고 난 뒤 다른 생각이 꼬리에 꼬리를 물고 끊임없이 일어난다. 관리능력을 풍대에 맡겼을 때, 우리의 의식은 영원한 씨앗인 채로 잠들게 되니 이것을 무의식無意識이라 부른다. 이곳의 구름이 사라질 때 우리의 하늘이 보인다.

111 **4대四大**는 물질을 구성하는 네 가지 기본요소로, 지地·수水·화火·풍風을 말한다.

112 **공대空大**는 사대 중 하나로 빈 공간적인 개념이다. 공대는 절대 비어서 공空이 아니다. 공이란 허공이 아닌 진공眞空을 말하고, 반야般若(빛)가 일곱 가닥으로 나뉜 자리를 공空이라 부른다. 여기에 의지하는 모든 존재는 실상實像이 아닌 허물虛物이기에 색즉시공色卽是空이라 부르는 것이다. 이곳에서 수행자는 모든 물질이 존재와 비존재非存在를 반복하는 것을 체험하게 된다.

113 **심식心識**은 인식하고 식별하는 마음의 작용을 뜻한다.

114 **무애연기無碍緣起**는 모든 존재가 서로 걸림없이 자재하되 상호 의존하고 있음을 말한다. 대표적으로 화엄사상의 십현무애연기법문이 있다.

115 **자각自覺**은 스스로 깨치는 것을 말한다. 여기에는 두 가지 방법이 있는데,

생활 모든 규준 있으므로 육대연기[116] 그 실상[117]을 깨친 것이 부처니라.

운주사 와불 일명 '부부 와불'이라 하는 이 석조불상은 자미두수(북극성)를 상징한다고 한다.(만유제법연기萬有諸法緣起)

참선과 같은 수행 방법은 자력적自力的인 면이 강한 반면에, 비로자나 부처님에게 원願을 세워 의지하는 방법은 타력적他力的인 면이 강하다.

116 육대연기六大緣起는 육대가 우주법계에 두루 가득하여 만유제법萬有諸法을 연기함을 말한다.

117 실상實相은 생멸무상生滅無常의 상相을 떠난 만유萬有의 진상眞相·진여眞如·본체本體를 뜻한다.

제11장 삼밀가지속질현[118]

무릇 육대체로 하여 연기하는 만상들은 그 상에서 당연하게 모든 작용 있으므로 이 작용을 신구의 삼밀이라 이름한다.

대저 불교 원래부터 인간종교임으로서 우주만유 모든 작용 신구의[119]에 비했으며, 현교에서 신구의를 삼

---

118 삼밀가지속질현三密加持速疾顯은 모든 중생은 3가지 가지력加持力, 즉 부처님의 가지력, 삼밀행三密行, 그리고 그것들간의 상호작용으로 빨리 부처가 될 수 있다는 이론이다.

119 신구의身口意에서 신身은 육체를 말하고, 구口는 말을 의미하고, 의意는 뜻을 의미한다.

업[120]이라 하였으나 밀교에는 신구의를 삼밀이라 이름하여 삼밀작용활동[121] 의해 성불한다 설하고, 현교에서 미혹迷惑되는 근본이라 이른 것을 밀교서는 깨쳐가는 근본이라 설하느니라. 삼업정화三業淨化 하는 곳에 삼밀행이 있음이니 이를 정화하려 하면 부처님의 가지력과 관행자[122]의 공덕력과 저법계의 통합력에 의지하지 아니하면 정화되지 않느니라. 공덕력은 삼밀로서 관행함에 있는지라, 불이 설한 진실한 일 실행함이 신밀[123]이요, 불이 설한 진실한 말 말씀함이 구밀[124]이

---

120 삼업三業은 신구의身口意에 의하여 나타나는 과업을 말한다. 사람은 몸과 입과 생각으로 업業을 짓는다. 이를 신구의 삼업이라고 한다.
121 삼밀작용행위三密作用行爲는 밀교 수행법의 하나로 신구의身口意의 3밀 행법이다. 즉 중생이 몸(손)으로 인印을 결하고, 입으로 진언을 외우고, 뜻으로 생각하는 실천법이다.
122 관행자觀行者는 위빠사나 수행을 통해 성인의 도에 이르는 수행자이다.
123 신밀身密은 3밀 중 하나로, 태도나 행위로 나타나는 것을 말한다. 불교의식에서 신밀에 해당되는 것으로 의식무용이 있다.
124 구밀口密은 3밀의 하나로 말이나 언행으로 나타나는 현상을 말한다. 우주간의 온갖 언어·음성의 활동을 어밀語密 또는 구밀口密이라 한다. 불교의식에서 구밀에 해당되는 것으로 진언과 다라니의 독송과 염불이 있다.

요, 불이 설한 진실한 맘 가지는 것 의밀[125]이라. 이와 같은 삼밀행위三密行爲 성불하는 길인 고로 삼밀가지 하게 되면 속히 나타나느니라.

이와 같은 삼밀작용 누구라도 가졌으며 축생아귀畜生餓鬼 지옥에도 모두 그러함으로써 이 법계가 정화되면 일체가 다 불인지라, 이 세간에 모든 만물 서로 관계 있으므로 제석천왕帝釋天王 몸에 달린 무수 보주寶珠 서로 비춰 중중제망[126] 일대미관一大美觀 이뤄짐과 다름없이 세간만사 서로 도와 장엄세계莊嚴世界 이뤄지니 이와 같은 장엄세계 불국정토佛國淨土 되느니라.

---

125 의밀意密은 3밀 중 하나로 의식적이고 정신적인 활동을 말한다. 부처님이 설한 진실한 마음을 가지는 것이다.

126 중중제망重重帝網은 보석이 촘촘히 엮어져 아름답게 빛나는 망을 뜻하며 시간·공간, 내면·외면, 정신·물질, 개인·전체, 인간·자연 등 어떻게 보아도 실상은 따로따로 분리·독립되어 있지 않다. 마치 "그물의 코처럼 서로 의지하고 도움을 주고받으며 존재하고 있다." 이를 『화엄경』에서 '제망중중무진연기帝網重重無盡緣起'라고 하였다.

제12장 자성법신[127]

비로자나 부처님은 시방삼세 하나이라 온 우주에 충만하여 없는 곳이 없으므로 가까이 곧 내 마음에 있는 것을 먼저 알라. 뜰에 심은 저 나무가 매일 자라나지마는 항상 보는 사람 눈에 안 보이는 것과 같이, 우리 심공[128] 과정에도 매일 성품 좋아지나 항상 보는 사람

---

127 **자성법신自性法身**은 비로자나불을 뜻하며 자성신과 같은 말이다. 법法·보報·응應의 3신 중 법신法身의 하나이다.
128 **심공心空**은 마음의 성품이 끝없이 넓고 커서 일체의 만상萬象을 다 포함한 것을 대허공大虛空에 비유한 것으로, 모든 장애가 사라진 공공적적空空寂寂한 심경을 뜻한다.

들은 좋아진 줄 모르고 오륙칠 년 지나보면 좋은 성품
性品 보일지라. 이 이치를 미리 알고 가족 간에 서로
도와 꾸준하게 불교를 믿고 성품 날을 지킬지라.

탁발 스님들이 발우를 들고 탁발하는 모습(미얀마)

제13장 현교와 밀교

불교에는 현교와 밀교의 두 갈래가 있으니 현교는 석가모니가 언어와 문자로 나타내어 설하신 교법이며, 밀교는 불법의 가장 심오한 진리로서 그 경지에 도달한 자만이 알 수 있는 비밀 문이다.

또한 밀교는 현교의 선사상禪思想, 미타사상彌陀思想, 관음사상觀音思想, 미륵사상彌勒思想 등이 모두 포함된 통합불교로서 발달했으며, 현세이익과 사후극락을 함께 얻는 종지宗旨로서 우주의 만법을 갖추지 않음이 없는 최상승의 법문이다.

과거 우리나라에도 신라시대 혜통대사惠通大師께서 전래한 후 궁중에서부터 일반 민중에게까지 밀교사상이 보급되었으며, 고려시대까지는 전성기를 만났으나, 조선시대에 와서 억불정책抑佛政策으로 인해 타종파와 통합되고 밀교 독특한 경전과 의궤儀軌는 모두 소각당하고 말았던 것이다.

현교는 심본색말[129]을 주장하니 미래 중심의 유심[130]적인 불교이므로 결국은 사후死後불교가 된다. 심본색말이란 뜻은, 현교에서 실상 모든 이치는 미묘하다고 근본이라 하여 앞세우고, 색상현실 모든 일은 허망하다고 끝이라 하여 뒤따르게 함을 말함이니, 한 이치에

---

[129] 심본색말心本色末은 마음을 근본으로 삼고 육체나 물질(色)은 말단(끝, 지말)이라고 하는 것으로, 즉 마음이 중심이 되고 사물은 그것에서 갈라져서 나온다는 것이다. 마음이 주체가 되고 물질은 그것에 부수적으로 따르는 주종의 관계라는 것이다.

[130] 유심唯心은 우주의 모든 존재는 마음의 표현이며, 이것을 떠나서 존재하는 것은 없고, 마음은 만물의 본체本體로서 유일한 실재라고 하는 화엄경의 중심사상이다.

서 모든 일이 벌어진다는 현교의 교리강령인 일원논리[131]이다. 밀교는 색심불이[132]를 주장하니 현세 중심의 현실적 실천불교이므로 결국은 생활불교가 된다.

색심불이의 뜻은 밀교에서 색상현실 모든 일은 곧 진리이며 실상으로 보아서 색을 품 안에 넣지 않고 이것이 이치라고 하는데, 물과 심이 평등해지는 고로 일체 세간 현상 그대로 불법과 일치함을 체득하는 밀교 교리 강령인 이원논리[133]이다.

밀교의 교주 법신부처님은 언제나 진실법으로서 중생을 교도하고 현교의 교주 화신부처님은 언제나 방편

---

131 **일원논리一元論理**는 우주의 본체는 유일한 것으로 사물의 다양성·잡다성을 이것에 귀일시키거나 또는 이것으로부터 이끌어낼 수 있다는 학설이다.
132 **색심불이色心不二**는 "색법色法과 심법心法이 둘이 아니다"라는 의미이다. 즉 유형有形의 물질과 무형無形의 정신이 같다는 뜻이다.
133 **이원논리二元論理**는 인간의 마음은 중생과 부처의 양면성을 나타내기 때문에, 중생과 부처는 둘이 아니라 하나인 일원론一元論이라고 할 수 있다.

으로써 중생을 교도하신다. 법신은 본래 방편을 쓰지 못하므로 때와 근기에 따라서는 당신이 곧 화신으로 화현하여서 방편법을 쓰게 되니 그러므로 화신불은 방편법을 쓰기 위해서 출세하신 부처님이라 만약 진실법을 쓰려면 도로 법신이 되어야 한다.

제14장 현교와 밀교도 하나 불교

현교밀교[134] 한 불교이지만 종지만은 다른지라, 이리 저리 가고 보면 생전극락 언제 가볼까. 이 종교 저 종교 한 진리이나 방편만은 다른지라, 이 문 저 문 열다 보면 성공할 날 없게 된다.

콩과 팥이 같은 식물 이름만은 다른지라, 한 그릇에 합쳐 보면 물건 가치 어디 있소. 저와 나와 같은 사람

---

134 **현교밀교**顯敎密敎에서 현교는 비밀이 없이 일반적으로 설한 교리이며, 밀교는 비밀히 설한 것으로 표면상으로는 알 수 없는 가르침이라는 뜻이다.

근기根氣만은 다른지라, 설왕설래 주저 말고 의지 따라 제도하자. 법신보신[135] 일체이나 명호만은 같지 않다. 청정원만 분화해야 대승[136]적이 발달되고 물과 심이 동체이나 양성만은 다른지라, 내 종지[137]를 세워야만 즉신성불 되어진다.

---

135 **법신보신法身報身**은 부처의 삼불신三佛身, 즉 법신法身·보신報身·화신化身 중 두 가지이다.
136 **대승大乘**은 '크게 타는 것'의 뜻으로, 미혹迷惑의 차안此岸으로부터 무상정등정각無上正等正覺의 피안彼岸에 이르는 교법을 말한다.
137 **종지宗旨**는 한 종파에서 가장 근본적이고 핵심적인 교리나 교의敎義를 말한다. 선종에서는 불법의 근본을 말한다.

제15장 화엄사상에서 비로자나불

화엄사상華嚴思想은 화엄경華嚴經을 소의경전所依經典으로 하여 정립된 사상이다. 화엄사상의 철학적 구조는 법계연기[138]이다. 우주의 모든 사물은 그 어느 하나라도 홀로 있거나 일어나는 일이 없다.

---

[138] 법계연기法界緣起는 『화엄경華嚴經』을 바탕으로 유심설唯心說에 근거하여, "모든 사물과 사상思象이 자재롭게 서로 의지하는 바가 되어, 한없이 교류하고 융합하여 일어나고 있음"을 나타낸다. 법계연기法界緣起는 '법계무진연기法界無盡緣起' 또는 '중중무진연기重重無盡緣起'라고도 한다.

모두가 끝없는 시간과 공간 속에서 서로의 원인이 되며, 대립을 초월하여 하나로 융합하고 있다는 것이 화엄에서 가르치는 무진연기[139]의 법칙이다. 사법계[140]· 십현연기[141]·육상원융[142]·상입상즉 등은 이무이진연기[143]를 설명하는 화엄사상의 골자이다.

사법계四法界는 현상과 본체와의 상관관계를 사법계·

---

139 무진연기無盡緣起는 법계연기와 같은 의미이다. 만물은 서로 인연이 얽혀 있으며, 상호의존함이 끝이 없음을 말한다.

140 사법계事法界는 형이상학적인 부처의 4세계四法界 중 하나이며, 『화엄경』에서 모든 사법事法은 서로 장애되지 않고 원융圓融하여 서로서로 인이 되고 연이 되어 한량없이 생겨나고 없어진다고 하는데 이것을 사법계라고 한다.

141 십현연기十玄緣起는 '십현문十玄門' 또는 '십현연기무애법문十玄緣起無礙法門'이라고 하며, 『화엄경』에 나타난 이론 중 하나로 육대무애六大無碍가 서로 작용하여 하나로 통합되는 것을 의미한다.

142 육상원융六相圓融에서 육상六相을 체상용體相用의 관계로 나누어 보면 총상總相과 별상別相은 연기의 체體라고 보고, 동상同相과 이상異相은 연기의 상相이라고 하고, 성상成相과 괴상壞相은 연기의 용用이라고 할 수 있다.

143 이무이진연기異無異塵緣起는 특정한 개체와 비 특정한 개체간의 원초적인 인연을 뜻한다.

이법계[144]·이사무애법계[145]·사사무애법계[146] 등 넷으로 나누어 설명한다. 모든 사물이 제각기 한계를 지니면서 대립하고 있는 차별적인 현상의 세계를 사법계라 하고, 언제나 평등한 본체의 세계를 이법계라 한다. 그러나 현상과 본체는 결코 떨어져서는 있을 수 없는 것이어서 항상 평등을 나타내고 있는데 이를 이사무애법계라 한다. 다시 나아가 현상, 그것도 각 현상마다 서로 서로가 원인이 되어 밀접한 융합을 유지한다는 것이 사사무애법계이다. 이 사사무애법계는 화엄사상의 특징을 나타낸 것으로, 일반적으로 중중무진[147]

---

144 이법계理法界는 청정심에 의해서 만들어진 시공과 주객을 초월한 세계이다. 사법계는 이법계가 시공을 초월하여 현상에 반연하여 일으키는 세계이다.
145 이사무애법계理事無碍法界는 사법계四法界 중의 하나이며, 이 법계法界는 본체계와 현상계가 둘로 떨어져 있는 것이 아니라, 전체 속에 개체가 있고, 개체 속에 전체가 있다는 하나의 걸림 없는 상호관계 속에 있음을 뜻한다.
146 사사무애법계事事無碍法界는 『화엄경』에서 설하는 불교교리이며, 모든 중생이 장애 없이 모든 개별적인 존재들은 서로를 포함하고 포함되어 조화를 이루면서 본체와 양상이 융합되는 것을 의미한다.
147 중중무진重重無盡은 화엄경에서의 1이 10이 되고 10이 1이 되는 이론으로,

의 법계연기라고 하며, 그 특징적인 모습을 열 가지로 나누어 설명하니 이를 십현연기문이라 한다.

화엄경에서 설하는 연화장세계는 현상세계와 본체, 또는 현상과 현상이 서로 대립하는 모습을 그대로 지니면서도 서로 융합하여 끝없이 전개하는 약동적인 큰 생명체라고 설명할 수 있다. 이 연화장세계에서는 항상 화엄경의 중심불인 비로자나 부처님이 대 광명을 비추어 모든 조화를 꾀하고 있다.

화엄경의 교주인 비로자나불은 모든 부처님의 진신인 법신불로서 보통사람의 육안으로는 형상이 없는 우주의 본체인 진여실상을 의미하는 것이다. 이 부처를 신이라고 하였을망정 평범한 색신이나 생신이 아니며, 갖가지 몸이 이것을 근거로 하여 나오게 되는 원천적인 몸을 뜻한다. 그러나 이 부처님을 형상화시

우주의 모든 것은 서로 얽혀 있으면서 하나로 융합되어 있다는 뜻이다.

킬 때는 천엽연화의 단상에 결가부좌結跏趺坐를 하고 앉아, 왼손은 무릎 위에 놓고 오른손은 가볍게 들고 있다.

불상의 화대 주위에 피어 있는 천 개의 꽃잎 하나하나가 백억의 국토를 표현한 것으로서, 이 부처님이 있는 세계의 공덕무량功德無量함과 광대 장엄함은 헤아릴 길이 없음을 조형화한 것이다. 또 큰 연화로 이루어져 있는 이 세계 가운데에는 우주의 만물을 모두 간직하고 있다.

청정과 광명이 충만되어 있는 이상적인 불국토인 이 연화장세계는 화장세계, 연화장장엄세계해라고도 한다. 이 세계에는 큰 연화가 있고 그 가운데 일체의 국토와 일체의 사물을 모두 간직하고 있기 때문에 연화장세계라 한다.

대적광전 앞 연꽃 연꽃 송이가 부처님의 연화장장엄세계의 일부를 연상하게 해준다(김해 수인사).

이 세계에 대해서는 『화엄경』과 『범망경梵網經』에서 각각 달리 설명하고 있지만 우리나라에서 이 두 경전의 설을 모두 채택하고 있다. 『화엄경』에서는 비로자나불의 서원과 수행에 의하여 현출된 이상적인 세계가 이 세계라고 보았다. 즉 세계의 맨 밑에 풍륜[148]이

---

148 풍륜風輪은 수미산須彌山을 버티고 있다는 삼륜三輪의 하나이며 삼륜의 가장 아래에 있다. 풍륜의 밑은 허공이다. 그 맨 아래의 풍륜을 평등주라 이름하고, 그 맨 위의 풍륜을 수승위광장이라 한다.

있고 그 위에 향수해[149]가 있으며, 이 향수의 바다 속에 한 송이의 큰 연꽃이 있는데, 이 연꽃 속에 함장되어 있는 세계를 연화장세계라 한다.

『범망경』에서는 비로자나불이 천여 개의 잎으로 된 연화대蓮花臺에 앉았는데 그 천여 개의 잎이 각각 한 세계이고, 비로자나불로부터 화현한 천의 석가모니불이 천 개 세계에 있고 한 세계마다 다시 백억 개의 나라가 있다. 이 백억의 나라 하나하나에 당시 석가모니불이 있어서 연화장세계에 대한 연구는 화엄종의 번성과 화엄사상의 전개에 힘입어 우리나라에서 크게 성행하였지만, 신앙적인 측면에서는 극락정토 사상이나 도솔천[150] 왕생설에 비하여 민간에서는 전승되지

---

149 **향수해香水海**는 향해香海라고도 하는데, 수미산을 둘러싸고 있는 내해內海는 모두 향수해라 하며 이에 연화장세계 향수해와 사바세계 향수해 두 가지가 있다.
150 **도솔천兜率天**은 욕계육천欲界六天의 넷째 하늘로 내외內外의 두 원院이 있는데, 내원은 미륵보살이 살면서 교화를 받지 못한 중생을 위하여 설법하며, 외원은 천중天衆의 환락 장소라 한다.

않았다. 이는 연화장세계가 법계연기설과 관련이 있어 그 이해가 쉽지 않았기 때문이다.

다만 『삼국유사三國遺事』의 사복설화에서 사복이 원효대사元曉大師와 함께 어머니의 장례를 치르고 나서 "옛날 석가모니불이 사라쌍수 사이에서 열반[151]하였는데, 지금도 그와 같은 이가 있어 연화장세계에 들려 하네" 하고 띠풀을 뽑은 뒤 송장을 업고 그 속으로 들어갔다고 하는 관련설화가 전해지고 있다.

연화장세계의 교주는 우주 전체를 총괄하는 비로자나불이다. 이는 비로자나불이 허공과 같이 끝이 없어서 어느 곳에서나 두루 가득 차 있음을 상징적으로 나타낸 것이다. 석가모니불을 응신으로 삼고 있는 비로자

---

151 열반涅槃은 산스크리트어 니르바나를 음역한 말이며, 모든 번뇌를 해탈하여 불생불멸의 법을 체득한 경지를 뜻한다. 수행을 통해 도달한 궁극적 경지를 불교에서는 해탈이나 열반이라 한다. 또는 부처나 보살 등이 이 사바세계를 떠나 법계로 돌아가는 것을 의미하기도 한다.

나불은 때와 장소 및 사람 등에 따라 가변성을 띠고 그 모습을 나타낸다. 미혹에 결박된 사람의 눈에는 보이지 않지만 일심으로 생각하고 맑은 믿음으로 의심하지 않으면 어디에서든지 그를 만날 수 있다고 한다. 즉 중생이 진심으로 기도하고 간절히 희구하는 바에 따라 그들의 생각이나 행위 경계에 따라 때를 놓치지 않고, 때를 기다리지 않고, 어느 곳, 어느 때에나 알맞게 행동하고 설법하며, 여러 가지 상이한 모습을 나타내는 것이다. 비로자나불은 항상 여러 가지 몸, 여러 가지 명호, 여러 가지 삶의 방편을 나타내어 잠시도 쉬지 않고 진리를 설함으로써 우리가 살아가는 삶의 현장에서 일체 중생을 제도하는 것이다. 그러나 화엄경 안에서의 비로자나불은 침묵으로 일관한다. 석가모니는 보리수菩提樹 아래에서 깨달음을 이루자마자 비로자나불과 일체를 이루게 되며, 그 깨달음의 세계를 보현보살[152]을 비롯한 수많

---

152 **보현보살普賢菩薩**은 부처님의 행원行願을 대변하는 보살이며, 문수보살文

통도사 대광명전과 미얀마 보리수 수만 겁의 세월 동안 우주법계연기로 대광명전 앞 활짝 핀 불두화와 무성한 보리수는 중생들의 인연 이어주네.

은 보살들이 비로자나불의 무량한 광명에 의지하여 설법하는 형식을 취하고 있다. 또한 비로자나불에 의해서 정화되고 장엄되어 있는 세계는 특별한 부처님의 세계가 아니라 바로 우리들 자신이 살고 있는 현실세계를 의미한다는 큰 특징을 가진다.

殊菩薩과 함께 석가모니불을 협시脇侍하는 보살이다. 문수보살이 여래의 왼편에서 여러 부처님의 지덕智德과 체덕體德을 맡고, 보현보살은 오른쪽에서 이덕理德과 정덕定德과 행덕行德을 맡는다. 또 문수보살과 함께 일체보살의 으뜸이 되어서 언제나 여래께서 중생을 제도하는 일을 돕고 널리 선양한다. 또 중생들의 목숨을 길게 하는 덕을 가졌으므로 보현연명보살 또는 연명보살延命菩薩이라고도 한다.

이 세계 속에 있는 우리가 법신불인 비로자나불에게 예배禮拜하고 귀의, 순종함으로써 부처님의 지혜 속에서 떠오를 현실계의 상황을 스스로의 눈에도 비치도록 하는 것이다. 그리고 이 비로자나불의 세계로 돌아가는 길은 보살행을 통해서 가능해진다. 이는 형체가 없는 비로자나불이 보살들의 사회적 실천에 의해서 형체 있는 것으로 화현하는 과정을 의미하는 것이며, 최고의 깨달음으로 향하는 보살행이 깨달음 그 자체인 비로자나불에게로 돌아가는 길인 것이다.

제16장 화엄세계

영산재 불교 전통 의식인 영산재 중 식당작법(한국 중요무형문화재 제50호, 유네스코 무형문화재로 2009년 등재)

부처님의 몸뚱이는 우주법계宇宙法界 아니 계신 곳 없으며 널리 사바 일체 중생 앞에 나투시어 숙겁 인연 따라 두루두루 감응하고 항상 여기 법계장엄 깨달음의 빛 있다네.

● 일권경[153]

나에게 한 권의 경이 있으나
종이와 먹으로 만든 것이 아니다.
펼쳐 보아도 한 글자도 없지만
항상 대 광명을 비춘다.

---

[153] 일권경一卷經은 중국 명나라 말기 홍자성洪自誠의 『채근담菜根譚』에 수록된 선시禪詩로 원문은 다음과 같다. 아유일권경我有一卷經 불인지묵성不因紙墨成 전개무일자展開無一字 상방대광명常放大光明

제17장 비로자나불상과 전각명

대한민국 사원寺院에서 비로자나불을 봉안奉安하고 있는 전각을 대적광전大寂光殿, 대광명전大光明殿, 화엄전華嚴殿, 보광전普光殿 또는 비로전毘盧殿이라 한다. 이런 전각의 명칭이 붙여질 경우에 보통 비로자나불 중심으로 좌우에 노사나불[154]과 석가모니불을 봉안한다. 그리고 비로전이나 화엄전이라 할 때 일반적으

---

[154] 노사나불盧舍那佛은 삼신불三身佛 중 보신불로 노자나불盧遮那佛이라 쓰기도 한다. 오랜 수행으로 무궁무진한 공덕을 쌓고 나타나신 부처님으로, 대적광전 등에는 주불로 청정법신 비로자나불을 모시고 좌보처로 원만보신 노사나불, 우보처로 천백억화신 석가모니불을 모신다.

로 비로자나 부처님만을 봉안하는 것이 상례이다. 법당 안의 비로자나불상은 주로 지권인을 하고 결가부좌 자세로 앉아 있다. 그러나 고려말기부터 이 지권인이 변형되어 왼손을 오른손으로 감싼 모습으로 표현하는 경우가 많았다. 비로자나불상 뒤에 비로자나불 후불탱화後佛幀畵가 봉안되는데, 이는 보통 화엄경의 설법 장면이다.

비로자나불 전각 명칭 대적광전(해인사), 대비로전(해인사), 적광전(해인사 백련암), 대광명전(통도사), 화엄전(영각사), 비로전(불곡사) 등으로 쓰인다.

＊비로자나 부처님께 관심을 가지신 모든 불자님들의 도움으로 이 책이 빛을 보게 되었습니다.

단기 4343. 10. 3
종일 합장

참고 문헌

고영섭·황남주. 『한영불교사전』. 서울: 신아사, 2010.
박상은 역주. 서울: 도솔, 1995. Hesse, Herman. *Siddhartha*. Translated by Hilda Rosner. a New Directions Book, 1946.
서윤길. 『한국밀교사상사』. 서울: 운주사, 2006.
신기철·신용철 편저. 『새 우리말 큰 사전』. 서울: 삼성출판사, 1979.
안진호. 『석문의범』. 창문사, 소화10년.
이기문 감수. 『새 국어사전』. 서울: 두산동아, 2000.
정법성. 『나의 길 50여년』. 충북 옥천군: 금강 문화, 1997.
주보연(편). 『밀교사전』. 서울: 홍법원, 1998.
진각교전(편). 『해인행』. 서울: 태광문화사, pp.66~84, 1990.
홍법원 편·전관응 대종사 감수. 『불교학대사전』. 서울: 홍법원, 1994.
International Dharma Instructors Association(1995). *Guide to Korean Buddhist Temples*. Seoul: ogye Order Publishing, 1995.
Paraskevopoulos, John. *Call of the Infinite: The Way of Shin Buddhism*. California: Sophia Perennis Publications, 2009.
Sogyal, Rinpoche. *The Tibetan Book of Living and Dying*. Patrick Gaffney and Andrew Harvey eds. New York: Harper Collins, 1994.
Internet(2011) Available:http://blog.daum.net/chan5906/8475964
Internet(2010)
    Available:http://en.wikipedia.org/wiki/Sambhogak%C4%81ya
Internet(2011)Available:http://preview.britannica.co.kr/bol/topic.asp?article_id=b25h2254a
Internet(2011) Available:http://www.dkoso pedia.com/wiki/Buddhism

The Vairocana (The Birojanabul)
in English

영어본 비로자나불

Translated by Choonki, Park, Ph.D.

Preface

It is almost 40 years since at several temples I took refuge in the *Vairocana*[1](the Cosmic Buddha) who is the *Dharmakáya-Buddha* and *Dharmakáya*.[2] Now I hope to

---

1 This is read as Birojanabul(毘盧遮那佛) in Korean. (Hereafter every word or term from Korean is underlined and the words from Sanskrit are italianized.) I think that most western interpreters and Sanskrit readers may take this term '*Vairocana*'(Cosmic Buddha), instead of 'the *Vairocana*,' on the base of Christianity. This paper, however, will take "*The Vairocana*" on the base of only Buddhism.

2 It may be referred to '**human beings' law**'(inkanpub: 人間法) on the view of western society. However, in the view of the oriental society it may mean '**natural law as well as human law**'(jayeanpub: 自然法 & inkanpub: 人間法). Thus, 'the dharma-body(bupshin: 法身)' is preferable. The Dharma*káya* Buddha(bupshinbul: 法身佛) comes from this term. It means the pure, shining body and clear appearance of the Buddha, who is the Vairocana. 'In Shin Buddhism, *Nirvana* or Ultimate Reality(also known as the "Dharma-Body"(法身) or *Dharmakáya* in the original Sanskrit) has assumed a more concrete

inform my dear human beings in *Sabhā* world of the great *Vairocana*'s infinite *Dharma*.[4] Needless to say, it

---

    form as ① the Buddha of Infinite Light (*Amitabha*) and Infinite Life (*Amitayus*) and ② the "Pure Land" or "Land of Utmost Bliss" (*Sukhavati*), the realm over which this Buddha is said to preside …. Amida is the Eternal Buddha who is said to have taken form as *Shakyamuni* and his teachings in order to become known to us in ways we can readily comprehend [John Paraskevopoulos, *Call of the Infinite: The Way of Shin Buddhism* (California: Sophia Perennis Publications, 2009), pp.16-7]. It is written as *Dharma-kāya* in Sanskrit which means "one of the 3 Embodiment Buddha Bodies or the only Buddha in the universe(bubshin: 法身)" [*The Encyclopedia of Buddhology,* ibid., p.512]. *Dhammakāya* is a Pāli word meaning "body of dharma" or the **body of enlightenment** [Internet (2010) Available: http://en.wikipedia.org/wiki/Dharma-kaya].

3 It is written as *Sabhā* world in Sanskrit which means "suffering land(sabasekye: 娑婆世界)" [*The Encyclopedia of Buddhology,* p.658.]. In Epic Sanskrit, the term also refers to an assembly hall or council-chamber, and to a hostel, eating-house, or gambling-house [Internet (2010) Available: http://en.wikipedia.org/wiki/Sabh%C4%81].

4 Dharma (bup: 法) represents the Vairocana's holly words and secrets. *Dhárma* in Sanskrit is a multivalent term of great importance in

would be very difficult to express the true *Dharma* of the *Vairocana* who is unimpeded by written words. In spite of my inability, it seems to me that informing all mankind of the *Vairocana's Dharma* in writing should be a more essential achievement and virtue[5] of Buddha than anything else. Thanks to the aids of the *Vairocana*'s infinite light and great compassion,[6] my Buddhist monk teachers, senior and junior monks, and fellow practitioner monks[7] with whom I have followed Buddha's teachings

---

Indian philosophy and religions. In the context of Hinduism, it means one's righteous duty, and a Hindu's dharma is affected by the person's age, class, occupation, and gender. In modern Indian languages it can be equivalent simply to *religion*, depending on context. The word *dharma* translates as *that which upholds or supports*, and is generally translated into English as *law*.... Dharma also refers to the teachings and doctrines of the founders of Buddhism and Jainism, the Buddha and *Mahavira*. In Buddhist philosophy, *dhamma/dharma* is also the term for "phenomenon" [Internet (2010) Available: http://en.wikipedia.org/wiki/Dharma].

5 The virtue of the Buddha(kongduck: 功德) leads Buddhist disciple to the path of becoming Buddha.
6 It (jabi: 慈悲) always gives laymen great happiness and piety that saves all of their sufferings.
7 Fellow practitioner monks(doban: 道伴) studied Buddhism together

together, I am able to edit *Vairocana's Dharma* in English as well as in Korean.

The *Vairocana* is the *Dharmakāya-Buddha*, the *Dharmakāya* or the manifestation of *Dharma*, who leads me to the paths of becoming a buddha[8] by truly awakening me to find my own being. He teaches us, "If our minds get to be clear and pure,[9] the Buddha will always appear

---

at the Buddha school.

8 The *Vairocana* leads us to becoming a buddha(sengbul: 成佛).
9 *Parisuddha; visuddha* in sanskrit means pure and clean or perfect clean free from evil and defilement (cheongjung: 淸淨)〔*Korean-English Buddhist Dictionary with Sanskrit and English Equivalents,* ibid., p.574〕. It is written as *suddha* in Sanskrit which means "to be purified from bad and agony" 〔*The Encyclopedia of Buddhology,* op cit., p.1542〕. Purity (*suddha*) is an important concept within much of Theravada and Mahayana Buddhism, although the implications of the resultant moral purification may be viewed differently in the varying traditions. The aim is to purify the personality of the Buddhist practitioner so that all moral and character defilements and defects (*kleshas* such as anger, ignorance and lust) are wiped away and *Nirvana* can be obtained 〔Internet (2010) Available: http://en.wikipedia.org/wiki/Purity_in_Buddhism〕.

to us everywhere without thought for the world of utmost joy: the pure land of *Amitābha* in the west (*sukhāvatī*)[10] or this bitter *dukkha*[11] in our mundane world."

With the advent of industrial society following the long period of an agricultural way of life, materialism has become more important than anything else. Mankind in the 21st century doesn't understand that they are just a small part of the earth, but have destroyed their

---

10 This is written as keukrack(極樂) in Korean [Hongbubwon ed., *The Encyclopedia of Buddhology* (Seoul: Hongbubwon, 1988), p.165]. *Sukhāvatī* (Sanskrit:*sukhāvatī*) refers to the western Pure Land of the Buddha Amitābha in Mahāyāna Buddhism. *Sukhāvatī* translates to "Land of Bliss [Internet (2010) Available: http://en.wikipedia.org/wiki/Sukh%C4%81vat%C4%AB].

11 *Dukkha* (gotong: 苦痛) (Sanskrit *dukkha*; according to grammatical tradition derived from *dus-kha* "uneasy", but according to Monier-Williams more likely a Prakritized form of *dus-stha* "unsteady, disquieted") is a Pali term roughly corresponding to a number of terms in English including suffering, pain, discontent, unsatisfactoriness, sorrow, affliction, anxiety, dissatisfaction, discomfort, anguish, stress, misery, and frustration [Internet (2010) Available: http://en.wikipedia.org/wiki/Dukkha].

environment in an immeasurable way. This earth now suffers from natural disasters more and more. Currently, we are reaping the benefits of the *karma*:[12] the law of cause and effect which means 'our actions' (the cycle of suffering and rebirth for each being) from our destruction of nature such as global floods, greenhouse effect on the weather and so on.

Although a lot of religious and political leaders claim to support love and philanthropy, most of their interests are to expand their own land as well as their concerns in this world where there are still unceasing wars. Besides, there are many proud but intelligent people who

---

12 *Karma* (koabo: 果報) is the retribution for good or evil deeds, implying that different conditions in this (or any) life are the variant ripening, or fruit, of seed sown in previous life or lives [*Korean-English Buddhist Dictionary with Sanskrit and English Equivalents, op cit.*, p.36]. "*Karma* from Sanskrit: "action, work" in Buddhism is the force that drives *sasara* - the cycle of suffering and rebirth for each being. Good, skillful deeds (Pāli: "*akusala*") actions produce 'seeds' in the mind which come to fruition either in this life or in a subsequent rebirth" [Internet (2010) Available: http://en.wikipedia.org/wiki/Buddhism].

rarely know both how to fully understand our complicated cycle of birth, aging, sickness, and death;[13] and how to live in true happiness. They are instead preoccupied with the rights and interests of the good, the sincere, and the underprivileged.

Nowadays there are three problems we have to solve as follows:

- The Harmony between Human beings and Nature;
- The Harmony between Religions; and
- The Harmony between Knowledge and our Way of Life.

The *Vairocana* as the *Dharmakáya-Buddha* as well as *Dharmakáya* or manifestation, has already provided us with the solutions by proposing his infinite and pure truth in the three celestial realms of Buddha World.[14]

---

13 This is written as sangrobeyungsa(生老病死) in Korean whose cycle is birth, aging, disease and death.

14 In Buddha world there are three celestial realms: a small celestial realm, a middle celestial ream, and a big celestial realm over the micro world where the human beings live(samchundaichun-

Now in order to make them listen to the sound of the *Vairocana*'s infinite *Dharma* until all lay living things[15] and the realm of space in Buddha world[16] have disappeared. Let's pray for not only all the laymen (all living things, including lay disciples) who can't see the *Vairocana*'s infinite teachings: the *Dharma* and Manifestation because of their 5 greedy desires[17] (*kāmaguna*:

<u>seikye</u>: 三千大天世界) [*The Encyclopedia of Buddhology*, op cit., p.778]. Someone translated it into 'three thousand great three-worlds' in Diamond Sūtra.

15 It (<u>jungshaeng</u>: 衆生) can be referred to as 'lay people or lay living things' in the universe that comprise from a small earthworm to a person even including a ghost in the hell. It is referred to as 'the 9 realms or the worlds in which all lay living things live'(<u>jungshaengkye</u>: 衆生界), except one Buddha realm [*The Encyclopedia of Buddhology*, ibid., p.1461].

16 It (<u>kongkye</u>: 空界) which is one of the Buddha realms: space, is referred to as 'everything looking like emptiness surrounded by the universe.' Through human beings' eyes it is seen as emptiness[*The Encyclopedia of Buddhology*, ibid., p.1668].

17 There are 5 greedy desires such as forms, sounds, odors, flavors, and tangibles; or wealth, sexuality, food, honorary, and sleeping [*The Encyclopedia of Buddhology* op cit., p.1112]. There is also craving for forms(<u>ohyouk</u>: 五慾) such as 'sounds, odors, flavors,

cravings) and 7 emotions;[18] but also the proud but intelligent people who because of too much pride are unprepared to lower their position, or misunderstand the natural flow of the mind like water flowing in a river.[19]

The *Vairocana*'s infinite and pure *Dharma* confirms to us the truth that the *Vairocana* is the Buddha of the micro universe. Like the sun or the moon the *Vairocana* casts light everywhere and over all the people who seek plants in the forest and water in the sea.

Currently these people should understand that all living things in the universe, such as a handful of soil, a plant, a blade of grass, and even a small earthworm, have a part of Buddha-nature.[20] Now is the time that

---

tangibles and mind-objects' [Internet (2010) Available: http://en.wikipedia.org/wiki/Outline_of_Buddhism].

[18] It means the 7 emotions(chiljung: 七情) that human beings have such as joy, anger, worry, horror, love, hate, and possession [*The Encyclopedia of Buddhology*, ibid., p.1578].

[19] It (whashim: 下心) represents modest human beings whose mind always likes to take a lower position rather than a higer one.

[20] It is referred to as "Buddha-nature or Buddha Principle(bupshinche:

we should give them great mercy as just one part of our lives. Thus, please let's pray for all the things that would be able to get Buddhahood.

The great *amvamramhamkham*[21] Variocana!

Worshipping with my hands clasped in prayer (*gassho*),[22]

法身體)" within Mahayana Buddhism, to be an intrinsic, immortal potential for reaching enlightenment that exists within the mind of every sentient(lay living) being. Buddha-nature is not to be confused with the concept of *Atman*, or Self, but instead is viewed to be empty of defining characteristics [Internet (2010): Available: http://en.wikipedia.org/wiki/Buddha-nature].

21 They are referred to as 5 meta cosmic elements: land, water, fire, wind, and emptiness which are the Dharma body of the Vairocana. They have two kinds of sound: yang and ying. Yang can be read as **avarahakha** instead of ying sound: **amvamramhamkham.**

22 "*Gassho*"(hapjang: 合掌) means a position used for greeting with the palms together and fingers pointing upwards in prayer position; used in various Buddhist traditions, but also used in numerous cultures throughout Asia. It expresses greeting, request, thankfulness, reverence and prayer [Internet (2010) Available: http://en.wikipedia.org/wiki/Glossary_of_Buddhism].

Buddhist Monk, Jongil[23]

---

[23] He (宗一: 1951- currently) is one of the Korean Buddhist Monks who is a joojee(住持: abbot: a master or head) of the temple of Bokyungsa(普鏡寺), Seongnam, Korea.

Introduction

From childhood, I greatly suffered from chronic illnesses that remained uncured through the whole gamut of natural remedies and medicines. At 22 years old, with the revelation of the Buddha I took refuge in the Kwansheiomboshal, the *Bodhisattva* of Compassion.[24] By sincerely worshipping I became a Buddhist Nun in October, 1958 on Mt. Youngchook located at Changyoungcounty, Kyungnam Province[25] in South Korea. There I did my best to pray all day and night

---

24 The Sanskrit term Bodhisattva(kwansheiomboshal: 觀世音菩薩) is the name given to anyone who, motivated by great compassion, has generated *bodhichitta,* which is a spontaneous wish to attain Buddhahood for the benefit of all sentient beings. What makes someone a Bodhisattva is her or his dedication to the ultimate welfare of other beings, as expressed in the prayer. [International Dharma Instructors Association, *Guide to Korean Buddhist Temples* (Seoul: Jogye Order Publishing, 1995), p.93.]

25 The province is located in the southern area of South Korea.

by either working while praying or praying while working. Thanks to the Kwansheiomboshal, the *Bodhisattva* of Compassion, on Mt. Youngchook, within less than one month I finally got over the chronic illness which had lasted for more than 20 years.

At that time, and in front of Buddha, I made up my mind to save all living things that are suffering from illness and took an oath, "If my own suffering can become all the others' well-being, I will try to do my best for their well-being." With only one thought on my mind (mindfulness)[26] and without sleeping day or night, I traveled around several temples praying and devoted myself to saving all things that are suffering.

In Daein Cave on one side of Mt. Youngchook,[27]

---

26 "Mindfulness(ilyumjungjin: 一念精進)" is the process of the practice whereby a person is intentionally aware of his or her thoughts and actions in the present moment, non-judgmentally [Internet (2010) Available: http://en.wikipedia.org/wiki/Mindfulness].

27 This mountain(youngchookshan: 靈鷲山) area is divided into two different local units naming mean: Kyesungmean and Youngshan-mean in Changyoungcounty, Kyungnam Province, South Korea.

Youngshanmean, the *Vairocana* Himself, the *Dharma-káya* or manifestation of *Dharma*, prophesied that I would be a buddha in the near future (Buddha's words that one becomes a buddha in his life or next life).[28] He touched me on the forehead, saying "Buddhist Nun, Pupsung, you are a student of Mine forever. From now on you preach your own *Dharma*/Buddhahood lessons by building a temple." For three months He had taught me how to get Buddhahood.

So far I have been teaching the *Dharma* of the *Vairocana*.

Worshipping with my hands clasped in prayer (*gassho*),

Duckodang, Pubsung[29]

---

[28] It's prophesied from Buddha which means "Someone will have to be the Buddha in his life." It is written as "shuki(授記) in Korean [*The Encyclopedia of Buddhology, op cit., pp.876-7*].

[29] She (法性: 1928-2005) was one of the great boshals(Buddhist nuns) as well as a joojee(abbot: a master or head) of the temple of Pubsungsa, Kyesungmean, Changyoung, South Korea.

I. The Vairocana and His Power

It is said that the *Vairocana* is the great illustrious Buddha[30] (Buddha of Illuminance-Reflection: the illumination of the *Amittabha* Buddha's virtue and truth for all lay living things)[31] as well as the Daeilyeorae-Buddha (*Mahā-vairocana*)[32] that is the great solar Buddha. As the solar

---

30 *Amitābha* Buddha saves all living things from suffering with infinite virtue light(kwangmyeungbyenjo: 光明遍照) that keep reciting Buddha's name [*The Encyclopedia of Buddhology*, ibid., p.113.].

31 All living things in the universe can be saved with the infinite virtue and light of the *Amittabha* Buddha(amittabul: 阿彌陀佛) [*The Encyclopedia of Buddhology*, ibid., p.1004].

32 It is called "the Birojanabul(毘盧遮那佛) or the Daeilyeorae(大日如來)" in Korea, which means the Sun. **Vairocana** (also **Vairochana** or **Mahāvairocana**) is a celestial Buddha who is often (e.g. in the Flower Garland Sūtra) interpreted as the Bliss Body of the historical *Gautama Buddha*; he can also be referred to as the Dharmakaya Buddha and the great solar Buddha [Internet (2010) Available: http://en.wikipedia.org/wiki/Vairocana].

light is similar to that of the *Vairocana*, it is called Daeilyeorae-Buddha.

The sun has three properties such as jeambyen-myung,³³ nuengsungjungmu,³⁴ and kwangmusangmeal.³⁵

---

33 It (jeambeunmyung: 除暗辨明) means that the virtue and wisdom light of the Daeilyeorae-Buddha can be everywhere in the universe, while the sun only casts light on the sunny area and day time, Thus, the Buddha light is more powerful than the sun light, which is called Daeilyeorae(大日如來) in Korea [Internet (2010) Available: http://edu.jingak.or.kr/view.php?bid=01_01&bno=20&start_num =0&bst=&chksort=1].

34 It (jungmu: 衆務) may mean that by the Buddha truth/dharma, more than 4 persons make decision to do something [*The Encyclopedia of Buddhology*, Ibid. p.1460]. Nuengsungjungmu(能成衆務) in Korean may be referred to as the mercy and virtue of the Buddha towards the lay sentient-beings. [Internet (2010) Available:http://edu.jingak.or.kr/view.php?bid=01_01&bno=20& start_num=0&bst=& chksort=1].

35 It (sangmeal: 生滅) is written "*utpādanirodha*" in Sanskrit which means birth and death, production and annihilation; all phenomena have birth and death, beginning and end, Namely, everything should pass away after being created in the universe like the sun light (kangmusaeingmeal: 光務生滅) [*The Encyclopedia of Buddhology*,

According to its three properties, the sun can cast light on the entire world through the darkness allowing all the things in the world to grow by virtue of the light. However, the solar light, in spite of its great virtue, has such limited power that it can cast light only by day, also it can be in a sunny area but it cannot be in the shade. If clouds are over the sun it can't work. It can't work at the bottom of deep seas or in caves. This solar light cannot cast both sides: darkness and light which cannot replace each other.

With the great power of virtue, however, the *Vairocana*'s infinite light has no restrictions, no limitation of day and night, no inside and outside, or no differentiation. It appears all over the world and saves all the living things from the deepest unknown agonies and darkness. His power illuminates the entire world and creates everything in the world. Thus, the *Vairocana* is the immortal and illuminating-creating Buddha.

Ibid. p.802]. However, it is referred to as the eternity truth of the Buddha [Internet(2010) Avaliable: http://edu.jingak.or.kr/view.php?bid=01_01&bno=20&start_num=0&bst=&chksort=1].

The *Vairocana* is the *Dharmakāya-Buddha*[36] that is the reasonable and rudimentary Buddha. So it is called truth in itself. Thus the *Dharmakāya-Buddha* has neither beginning nor end. The *Dharmakāya-Buddha* being both eternal and immortal has neither shape nor figure. However, in the 8th century, the Buddha Statue with jikwonin[37] (the shape of Buddha's holding fingers: with the left hand covered the right one or reversely) became an object of worship by all of us. Despite the fact that not all the Buddhas in oriental society have the name of the *Vairocana*, all the Buddhas were formulated as the

---

36 The Vairocana is also referred to as the *Dharmakáya* Buddha (bupshinbul: 法身佛) and the great solar Buddha. Buddhas are manifestations of the *Dharmakáya* called Nirmanakáya (ungwhabul: 應化佛). Unlike ordinary unenlightened persons, Buddhas (and arhats) do not die (though their physical bodies undergo the cessation of biological functions and subsequent disintegration) [Internet (2010) Available: http://en.wikipedia.org/wiki/Vairocana and http://en.wikipedia.org/wiki/Dharmak%C4%81ya].

37 The Daeil Yeorae Buddha(大日如來佛) in Kumkang Sūtra(金剛經: *vajraprajñā-pāramita-sūtra*) hold fingers hands together explaining oneness of both the Buddha and lay living things(jikwonin: 智拳印) [*The Encyclopedia of Buddhology, op cit.*, p.1477].

Vairocana that is truth and *Dharma*.

The *Vairocana* has such properties as:
- inherent own nature (*svabhāva*),[38]
- mind,
- Buddha,
- intrinsic body,[39]
- creator (mañju),[40]
- all the things in the universe,[41]

---

38 Svabhāva (jashung: 自性) may be referred to as the inherent own nature of every living thing [*The Encyclopedia of Buddhology*, p.1344]. "***Svabhāva***(IAST: *svabhāva*): *sabhāva*; Tibetan: ; Wylie: *rang-bzhin*) is intrinsic nature, essential nature or essence. The concept and term *svabhāva* are frequently encountered in Dharmic traditions such as Advaita Vedānta, "To become Brahman is to become highest self-nature (*sabhāva*)" (Atthakanipata-Att. 5.72) [Internet (2010) Available: http://en.wikipedia.org/wiki/Svabh%C4%81va].

39 It (bonchei: 本體) may mean "radical, fundamental, original, or one's own body."

40 It (manju: 萬有) means everything in the university that creator(the *Vairocana*) makes [*The Encyclopedia of Esoteric Buddhism*, p.228].

41 It is written as samramanshang(森羅萬象) in Korean which means everything in the universe.

- and Buddha world/land (*dharmadhātu*).⁴²

Thus, his principle can be realized 'as either one is all or all is one.'⁴³ If all the things in the universe are the embodiment or epiphany⁴⁴ of the *Vairocana*, there

---

42 It is written as '*dharmadhātu*' (bupkye: 法界) in Sanskrit which may be referred to as one of the 18 realms of Buddha world [*The Encyclopedia of Buddhology,*. p.500]. "Part of that knowledge is that all dharmas (things) have their basis in the *dharmadhatu* - the Totality of all that is, the All. In this sense, there is non-duality that characterizes everything, since everything is possessed of the 'one flavour' of the *dharma-dhatu*. The Buddha states: 'A bodhisattva knows that all dharmas rest eternally on the fundamental element (dharmadhatu) without coming or going [Internet(2010) Available: http://en.wikipedia.org/wiki/Shurangama_Samadhi_Sūtra]. *Dharmadhatu* (Sanskrit) may be defined as the 'dimension', 'realm' or 'sphere' (dhatu) of Dharma and denotes the collective 'one-taste' (Sanskrit: *ekarasa*) dimension of Dharmata [Internet (2010) Available: http://en.wikipedia.org/wiki/Dharmadhatu].

43 In Buddhism there is a theory "One can be all and all can be one". Thus, everything can be oneness which has originality dependence.

44 In Sino-Japanese Buddhism, the Vairocana is also seen as the embodiment of the Buddhist concept of *shunyata* or emptiness

is nothing but the *Vairocana* in the universe. Therefore, the *Vairocana* who is the pure Buddha, the truth in itself, the most basic principle of universal truth, transcends all religious theories/parties. The universe is the truth and the truth in itself is the living *Dharmakāya-Buddha* (*Dharma*-body).

The *Dharmakāya-Buddha* is the universal truth in itself as well as the body of all kinds of Buddhas. The *Dharmakāya-Buddha* who cannot be expressed as a concept or a thing always exists all around the universe as the unchanged truth. It should be acquired through the achievement of meditation[45] which is only acquired through hard practice and meditation. Namely, by both

---

as an epiphany (hyeunhyeun: 顯現)) [Internet (2010) Available: http://en.wikipedia.org/wiki/Vairocana].

45 "The way of learning to meditate yourself (jungduck: 證得) is the greatest gift you can give yourself in this life. For it is only through meditation that you can undertake the journey to discover your true nature, and so find the stability and confidence you will need to live, and die, well. Meditation is the road to enlightenment" [Rinpoche Sogyal, *The Tibetan Book of Living and Dying* (Patrick Gaffney and Andrew Harvey eds. New York: Harper Collins, 1994)].

getting enlightenment[46] and removing ignorance[47] one will get wisdom and see the *Dharmakāya-Buddha*. The reason is that the land of infinite patience *sabhā* in itself can be changed into the pure Bliss Land of Buddha (*Amitabha*-Buddha's Pure Bliss Land)[48] with enlightenment.

---

[46] It (junggak: 正覺) may be referred to as "awakening or enlightenment or the moment of becoming the Buddha" [*The Encyclopedia of Buddhology,op cit.*, p.1392].

[47] It (mumyeung: 無明) is written as *avidyā* in Sanskrit which may mean ignorance [*The Encyclopedia of Buddhology,* ibid., pp.401-2.]. "*Avidyā* is a Sanskrit word that means "ignorance", "delusion", "unlearned", "unwise" and that which is not, or runs counter to, vidya [Internet (2010) Available: http://en.wikipedia.org/wiki/Avidy%C4%81].

[48] It (kurakjungto: 極樂淨土) is the land of Ahmeetah-bool/*Amitabha* Buddha, Buddha of the Western Paradise. *The Encyclopedia of Buddhology,* p.166. *Amitābha* is the principal Buddha in the Pure Land sect, a branch of Buddhism practiced mainly in East Asia, while in *Vajrayana Amitābha* is known for his longevity attribute and the aggregate of distinguishing (recognition) and the deep awareness of individualities. According to these scriptures, *Amitābha* possesses infinite merits resulting from good deeds over countless past lives as a bodhisattva named *Dharmakāra*. "Amitābha" is translatable as "Infinite Light," hence *Amitābha* is

The Pure Bliss Buddha Land exists in individual human beings as well as in the occidental realm of Buddha Land, which can only be realized by themselves, not with other's aid or help. As everything converges on becoming enlightened, all the Buddhists do so on the *Variocana*. This world of the *Variocana* is that of the Grand Lotus Pure Land of Buddha.[49]

The Grand Lotus Pure World in itself is the land of the Buddha. The *Variocana* is the Buddha that always teaches the three celestial realms of unchanged Buddha World. As a highest and almighty Buddha, the Buddha only influences his teachings on the universe. All kinds of Buddhas appear as an embodiment of the *Variocana* and give life to the lay living things and teach them His lessons as well as His *Dharma*. Thus, the *Variocana* is the head of all kinds of Buddhas and the living Buddha.

---

    often called "The Buddha of Infinite Light" [Internet (2010) Available: http://en.wikipedia.org/wiki/Amitabha_Buddha].

49 It (yenwhajangjangoam: 蓮華藏莊嚴) is referred to as "the world like lotus in *Avantamsake Sūtra*" [*The Encyclopedia of Buddhology*, ibid., pp.1070-1].

The *Variocana* exists in the central celestial realm of Buddha Land[50] and his power is almighty as well as infinitely huge,[51] and his mind and body are pure and clean like the color of gold whose true light fills Buddha land. His almighty power and prestige casts light on all things in the universe and creates all kinds of things, saving the laymen from all diseases and suffering, eliminating evils, and helping the prayers to accomplish their wishes. That is to say, in harmony with each other as his name and title which contain its meaning, the *Variocana* is the sun and the moon. All kinds and shapes of things in the world are from the *Vairocana*'s power as well as the harmonious illumination[52] of the living Buddha.

---

50 It (sebanjungto: 西方淨土) is referred to as the Vairocana's postion in the Lotus Land of Buddha. It is not the real space but the Buddha's world where the *Vairocana* stays [*The Encyclopedia of Buddhology*, ibid., p.1718].

51 It (kangdaimubyeun: 廣大無邊) means the endless wide and large oneness like Buddha's teachings [*The Encyclopedia of Buddhology*, ibid., p.111, & 404].

52 Buddha's infinite light and brightness (kwangmeangjowha: 光明調化) can save all lay living things.

II. The Vairocana-10 Aspects of His Buddhakāya[53]

① In the central celestial realm of Buddhism Land, there is the *Variocana*, the Buddha God of purity and air, who freely governs all the shapes and aspects[54] over the celestial realms of Buddhism.[55]

---

53 It (shipshinbul: 十身佛) means that the *Variocana* can be changed as 10 aspects of the *Buddhakāya* [*The Encyclopedia of Buddhology,* ibid., p.965].

54 It (hyengsang: 形相) is written as '*rūpāvacara*' in Sanskrit which may mean human beings' face and appearance [*The Encyclopedia of Buddhology,* ibid., p.1685]. "Sense experience" (kāma), while *mahaggata* refers to the higher planes of forms (rūpāvacara) and formlessness (arūpāvacara)" [Internet(2010) Available: http://en.wikipedia.org/w/index?title=Special%3ASearch&search=r%C3%BBp%C4%81vacara&button=%3CIMG+alt%3DSearch+src%3D%22http%3A%2F%2Fbits.wikimedia.org%2Fskins-1.5%2Fvector%2Fimages%2Fsearch-ltr.png%3F283w%22%3E&fulltext=1].

55 Since the realms of Budda Land is separated from falsehood or untruth, it (jinbubkye: 眞法界) is a real realm of Buddha Land [*The*

② Only the *Variocana* has great and powerful light that cannot be stopped by anything or anybody.

③ The Great *Variocana*, the Buddha Body of profound form, of infinite pure virtue and goodness,[56] saves all the lay living things from evil.

④ The *Variocana* creates everything from the Land of Buddhism by His will and mind.

⑤ The *Variocana* harmoniously creates all kinds of forms, shapes and figures as many myriads as of dust.

⑥ The *Variocana* with great power teaches all the lay living things the truth on every mountain and in every river according to the divine inspiration between lay living things and the Buddhas.[57]

⑦ The *Variocana*, the *Nirmanakāya-Buddha*,[58] is

Encyclopedia of Buddhology, ibid., p.1501].

56 All of the good deeds bring happiness and pleasure(bokduck: 福德) [*The Encyclopedia of Buddhology*, ibid., p.559].

57 It (kamyeoung: 感應) means "the fused feeling between lay living things' feeling and Buddha's inspiration like empathy which can exist between man and Buddha" [*The Encyclopedia of Buddhology*, ibid., p.24].

58 *Nirmanakāya* (whashingbul: 化身佛 or yeungwhabul: 應化佛) is one Buddha of the Three *Buddhakāyas* (Buddha Bodies) who saves

transformed from all kinds of Buddhas with perfect freedom.⁵⁹

⑧ The *Variocana*, the body of wisdom, has the profound wisdom that broadly enlightens the entire world with bright light and the bright prospect of wisdom.

⑨ At each Buddhist school,⁶⁰ the *Variocana*, one linear body of the *Dharmakāya-Buddha*, lets both His body and wisdom act together.

⑩ The *Variocana* has the body of setting and original *karma*⁶¹ that can perform His mysterious power all over the world without moving.

The *Variocana* overcomes every obstacle and

---

all lay living things [*The Encyclopedia of Buddhology*, ibid., p.1712].

59 "One of the virtues that Buddha has is a kind of almighty (jajai: 自在)" [*The Encyclopedia of Buddhology*, ibid., p.1351].

60 It can commonly be read as 'dochang(道場) in Korean for Buddha school, instead of 'doryang' specially for Buddha text [*The Encyclopedia of Buddhology*, ibid., p.303].

61 'The animated/sentient body' can be obtained by rewarding the past *karma* (jungboyeibo: 正報依報)" [*The Encyclopedia of Buddhology*, ibid., p.1232].

illuminates this universe with all kinds of harmonious and enormous virtue. He enlightens the entire world with great thought by the 10 embodied kinds of inward and outward *Buddhakāya* such as:

- the land;[62]
- the lay living things;

---

[62] It (kukto: 國土) is written as '*ksetra*' in Sanskrit which may mean 'land, area, or the place that animals can live' [*The Encyclopedia of Buddhology*, p.154]. Mount Meru is at the centre of the world surrounded by *Jambūdvīpa*, in form of a circle forming a diameter of 100,000 *yojanas*. *Jambūdvīpa* continent has 6 mighty mountains, dividing the continent into 7 zones (Ksetra). The names of these zones are: *Bharat Kshetra, Mahavideh Kshetra, Airavat Kshetra, Ramyak, Hairanyvat Kshetra, Haimava Kshetra, and Hari Kshetra*. The three zones i.e. *Bharat Kshetra, Mahavideh Kshetra and Airavat Kshetra* are also known as *Karma bhoomi* because practice of austerities and liberation is possible and the *Tirthankaras* preach the *Jain* doctrine. The other four zones, Ramyak, *Hairanyvat Kshetra, Haimava Kshetra and Hari Kshetra* are known as *akarmabhoomi or bhogbhumi* as humans live a sinless life of pleasure and no religion or liberation is possible [Internet(2010) Available: http://en.wikipedia.org/wiki/Jambudvipa].

- the body of *karmic*-retribution according to the deeds of a former life;[63]
- the body of the hearing novice monk (*srāvaka*);[64]
- the self-realized Buddha (*pratyeka*-buddha);[65]

---

[63] 'The *karama* body (yepboshin: 業報身) is obtained by the previous bad *karma* or one Buddha from 10 aspects of the Buddha in *Avantamsake Sūtra* [*The Encyclopedia of Buddhology, op cit.*, p.1047].

[64] It is written as *srāvaka* in Sanskrit which may mean "the persons who can hear from their students(seoungmun: 聲聞)" [*The Encyclopedia of Buddhology*, p.846]. **Śrāvaka** or *Shravaka* (Sanskrit) or **Sāvaka** (Pāli) refers to "a hearer" or, more generally, "disciple." This term is used by both Buddhists and Jains. In *Jainism*, a shravaka is any lay J*ain*. Thus the term shravaka has been used for the Jain community itself (for example see Sarak and Saraogi). In Buddhism, the term is sometimes reserved for distinguished disciples of the Buddha [Internet (2010) Available: http://en.wikipedia.org/wiki/%C5%9Ar%C4%81vaka].

[65] It is written as *pratyeka-buddha* in Sanskrit which may mean "self-realized Buddha(yeongak: 緣覺)" [*The Encyclopedia of Buddhology*, p.1062]. A *Pratyekabuddha* or *Paccekabuddha* literally "a lone Buddha" , "a Buddha on their own" or "a private Buddha", is one of three types of enlightened beings according to some schools of Buddhism. The other two types are the

- the Buddhist Body (*Bodhisattva* of Body);[66]
- the *Dharmakāya* of the *Vairocana*;
- and as the body of air Buddha Body (the *Sūnya* Body)[67] that controls everything in the air.

Śrāvakabuddhas and *Samyaksambuddhas*. *Pratyekabuddhas* are said to achieve enlightenment on their own, without the use of teachers or guides, according to some traditions by contemplating the principle of dependent arising. They are said to arise only in ages where there is no Buddha and the Buddhist teachings (Sanskrit: dharma; Pāli: *dhamma*) are lost. Many may arise at a single time. Unlike Supreme Buddhas (see bodhi), their enlightenment is not foretold.

[66] "One of the 10 aspects of the Buddha(boshalshin: 菩薩身) in *Avantamsake Sūtra* may be a Buddha."

[67] It is written as *sûnyatā* in Sanskrit which means "the air controller of Buddha(hegongshin: 虛空身)" [*The Encyclopedia of Buddhology*, p.1669]. *Śūnyatā*,(Sanskrit noun from the adj. *śūnya*: "zero, nothing"), *Suññatā* (Pāli; adj. *suñña*), *stong-pa nyid* (Tibetan), *Kòng/Kū*, 空 (Chinese/Japanese), *Gong-seong*, (kongseoung: 空性) (Korean), *qoyusun* (Mongolian) is frequently translated into English as *emptiness*. *Sunya* comes from the root *svi*, meaning swollen, plus *-ta* -ness, therefore Conze glosses *sunya* as *hollow* (- ness). A common alternative term is "voidness" [Internet (2010) Available: http://en.wikipedia.org/wiki/%C5%9A%C5%ABnyat%C4%81].

III. The *Dharmakāya-Buddha*

As the *Variocana* is called the *Dharmakāya-Buddha*, so is *Sakyamuni* the *Nirmanakāya*. The Buddha truth that *Sakyamuni* awakens is that of the previous Buddhas, so the Buddha truth is but one in the universe as the same inherent phenomenon. Namely, even if *Sakyamuni* and all the previous Buddhas were not awakened to the truth, the universe would exist as the same truth that cannot be changed.

Such unchanged *Dharma*[68] in itself goes into the body of Buddha that gets to accord with Buddhism *Dharma*, which means actual body experience[69] is much better than just awakening oneself.[70] That is, only a human

---

68 It (bubyeunbup: 不變法) means unchangeable dharma.
69 The Buddha truth which can be obtained by one's actual body experience(cheduck: 體得).
70 It is written as *Buddha* in Sanskrit which means 'awakened-one'(gak:

being by himself gets to become enlightened with Buddhism truth, instead of acquiring it from others.

The Buddha's truth that originally has neither beginning nor end is one thing that exists forever as unchanging truth, which is the truth of Buddha. There appears *Sakyamuni* with a piety that saves all living things that don't know the truth of Buddhism, which is called *Sakyamuni* Buddha. According to this truth, as there is no Buddha except the *Variocana*, *Sakyamuni*-Buddha is transformed as the *Variocana* for the safety of all lay living things.

覺) that is a Buddha [*The Encyclopedia of Buddhology,* op cit., pp.13-4].

The View of Daijurkwhangjurn and Great Birojurn

Located on Mt. Gaya, Haeinsa Temple (one of the 3 major temples in Korea) has these 2 halls whose Varionaca Statues are dedicated.

IV. The *Sambhokāya* (*Rocana*)[71]

If anyone practices and prays for will, resolve, or desire (*pranihita*)[72] singlemindedly enough, they are able to become a buddha with the rewards of the *karma*. There were a lot of Buddhists before the era of *Sakyamuni* such as:

- *Amitabha*-Buddha (the Western Buddha Pure Land),
- Pagoda-Buddha (*Prabhūtaratna*)[73]

---

71 *Shambhokāya* (boshinbul: 報身佛) may be referred to as another name of the '*Rocana*, the Delighted-body Buddha' [*Guide to Korean Buddhist Temples*, op cit., p.93. and *The Encyclopedia of Buddhology*, op cit., p.341]. *Shambhokāya* also refers to one of the Buddha Bodies [*The Encyclopedia of Buddhology*, ibid., pp.549-50].

72 It (Won: 願) means the original prayerful resolution of desires for becoming a Buddha.

73 It is wirtten as '*Prabhūtarana*' which is the master of Oriental paradise of Buddha Land(dabuyeraie: 多寶如來). *The Encyclopedia of Buddhology*, op cit., p.235. 'Dabo (*Prabhutaratna*)', a buddha who

- and Medicine-Buddha.⁷⁴

All of them became the *Sambhokāya* with the single goal of saving lay people or lay living things.

Tongdosa Temple Built by Jajang Yulsa (590~658 AD) in 646 AD, it is known both for the biggest main temple and as one of the three treasure temples in Korea.

---

had already achieved enlightenment, riding the Tower of Many Treasures, appeared to attest to the validity of *Sakyamuni*'s sermons at Vulture Peak. Dabo and *Sakyamuni* then sat side by side within the tower [Internet (2010) Available: http://en.wikipedia.org/wiki/Dabotap].

74 It is written as yaksayeraie(藥師如來: *Bhaisajya-guru*) in Korean [*Guide to Korean Buddhist Temples*, p.93].

V. The *Nirmānakāya* (*Shakyamuni*)-the Transformed *Buddhakāya*

As the *Variocana* is called the *Dharmakāya-Buddha*, so is *Sakyamuni*-Buddha the *Nirmanakāya*. If you want to know the *Dharmakāya-Buddha*, first of all, you should see the three transformed *Buddhakāyas* from the *Variocana*.[75]

---

75 It (samshin: 三身) means three Buddha Bodies [*The Encyclopedia of Buddhology*, pp.751-2]. The *Trikaya* doctrine (Sanskrit, literally "Three bodies"; (samshin: 三身) Chinese: *Sānshēn*, Japanese: sanjin) is an important Buddhist teaching both on the nature of reality, and the nature of a Buddha. By the 4th century the Trikāya Doctrine had assumed the form that we now know. Briefly, the doctrine says that a Buddha has three *kayas* or *bodies*: the nirmanakāya or *created body* which manifests in time and space; the sambhogakāya or *body of mutual enjoyment* which is a body of bliss or clear light manifestation; and the Dharmakāya or *Truth body* which embodies the very principle of enlightenment and knows no limits or boundaries [Internet (2010) Available:http://

The reason why *Sakyamuni* left home and practiced asceticism[76] was to teach the laymen how to practice and avoid the cycling pains of birth, ageing, sickness, and death. Likewise, the reason why *Sakyamuni* was transiently transformed as a Statue of *Nirvana*[77] in the forest of the *Bodhi* tree[78] was to show the laymen what

---

en.wikipedia.org/wiki/Sambhoga-kaya].

[76] **Asceticism** (kumyouk: 禁慾) from the Greek: *áskēsis*, "exercise" or "training" in the sense of athletic training) describes a lifestyle characterized by abstinence from various sorts of worldly pleasures often with the aim of pursuing religious and spiritual goals [Internet(2010) Available: http://en.wikipedia.org/wiki/Asceticism].

[77] It (yeoulbanshang: 涅槃相) means when a Buddhist reached Buddhahood [*The Encyclopedia of Buddhology*, op cit., pp.1073-4].

[78] It (borhisoo: 菩提樹)) is a three where *Sakyamuni* got awakened under this tree [*The Encyclopedia of Buddhology*, ibid., p.646]. The ***Bodhi* Tree**, also known as *Bo* (from the Sinhalese Bo), was a large and very old Sacred Fig tree (*Ficus religiosa*) located in *Bodh Gaya* (about 100 km (62 mi) from Patna in the Indian state of Bihar), under which *Siddhartha Gautama,* the spiritual teacher and founder of Buddhism later known as Gautama Buddha, achieved enlightenment, or Bodhi [Internet (2010) Available: http://en.wikipedia.org/wiki/Bodhi_Tree].

uncertainty (*anitya*)[79] is like. Though it has temporally disappeared, the Buddha in itself[80] is unchanged as all of the Buddhas in this world are a form of the *Nirmanakāya* through transformation.

---

[79] It is wirtten as *anitya* in Sankrit which refers "both mind and things are so changeable that they cannot exist forever(musang: 無常)" [*The Encyclopedia of Buddhology,* p.405.]. Impermanence (Pāli: *anicca*; Sanskrit: *anitya*; Tibetan: *mi rtag pa*; Chinese: 無常 wúcháng; Japanese: 無常 mujō; Thai: anitchang, from Pali "anicca ŋ ") is one of the essential doctrines or Three marks of existence in Buddhism. The term expresses the Buddhist notion that all of conditioned existence, without exception, is in a constant state of flux. The Pali word anicca literally means "inconstant", and arises from a synthesis of two separate words, 'Nicca' and the "privative particle" 'a'. Where the word 'Nicca' refers to the concept of continuity and permanence, 'Anicca' refers to its exact opposite; the absence of permanence and continuity [Internet (2020) Available: http://en.wikipedia.org/wiki/Anitya].

[80] It (jinshin: 眞身) refers to the true body of the Buddha [*The Encyclopedia of Buddhology,* p.1503].

VI. The Originality of the *Dharmakāya-Buddha*

As the *Dharmakāya-Buddha* that inherently exists refers to the mind of *bodhi* (*bodhi-cittava* which means the mind of awakening to be a buddha),[81] so does the *Nirmanakāya-Buddha* that appears through practice to the action of *bodhi*.[82]

---

81 It is written as '*bodhicittava*'(borhishim: 菩提心) in Sankrit which means "In Buddhism, a *bodhisattva* (Sanskrit: *bodhisattva*; Pali: *bodhisatta*) is either an enlightened (bodhi) existence(sattva) or an enlightenment-being or, given the variant Sanskrit spelling *satva* rather than *sattva*, "heroic-minded one (satva) for enlightenment (bodhi)." Another term is "wisdom-being." It is anyone who, motivated by great compassion, has generated bodhicitta, which is a spontaneous wish to attain Buddhahood for the benefit of all sentient beings" [Internet (2010) Available: http://en.wikipedia.org/wiki/Bodhisattva].

82 (Borhihyeong: 菩提行) See [*The Encyclopedia of Buddhology, op cit.*, p.537].

As the *Dharmakāya-Buddha* becomes the *Nirmanakāya*-Buddha for the safety of all the laymen, there is no Buddha but *Dharmakāya-Buddha* in this universe.

The *Dharmakāya-Buddha* is like the sun and the *Nirmanakāya* is like the full moon. Thus, the *Variocana* in accordance with the name and title of Buddha,[83] is just the Buddha: the Solar Great Buddha (*Mahāvarocana*).

As the esoteric holy words (*vajrayāna*)[84] that inherently represents Yang[85] the *Dharmakāya-Buddha*'s aims are

---

83 It is "the title or name of Buddha(bupshinmyeongho: 法身名號)" [*The Encyclopedia of Buddhology,* ibid., pp.380-1].

84 It is written as *vajrayāna* which may mean "the opposite meaning of the written holy words by *Sakyamuni* Buddha(milkyo: 密敎)" [*The Encyclopedia of Buddhology,* ibid., p.440]. *Vajrayana* is a complex and multifaceted system of Buddhist thought and practice which evolved over several centuries and encompasses much inconsistency and a variety of opinions [Internet (2010) Available: http://en.wikipedia.org/wiki/Vajrayana].

85 Yang(陽), in yin(陰) and yang, is the word for one half of the two opposing forces in Chinese philosophy, described as "bright positive masculine principle" in Chinese dualistic cosmology

mainly

- to purify the present world;[86]
- to wish for actual safeness in this world;[87]
- to make this earth purified;[88]
- to pray for safeness of nations;[89]
- to recite Buddhism words (*sāntika*)[90] both to avoid all kinds of suffering and to become a self-enlightened Buddha;[91]

[Internet (2010), Available: http://en.wikipedia.org/wiki/Yang].

86 It (hyeanshei: 現世) means current world where there is a lot of suffering and agony [*The Encyclopedia of Buddhology*, op cit., p.1679].

87 It (hyeansheianrack: 現世安樂) refers to another name of Bliss Land of Buddha [*The Encyclopedia of Buddhology*, ibid., p.1024].

88 The Buddha Land (jeungto: 淨土) where there is great enlightenment and happiness, whereas this mundane world is full of poverty, disease, and suffering [*The Encyclopedia of Buddhology*, ibid., pp.1408-9].

89 "A nation is governed by the Buddha Truth or Principle (jhinhokukka: 鎭護國家)" [*The Encyclopedia of Buddhology*, p.1511].

90 It is written as *sāntika* in Sankrit which means that "human beings can be saved from all kinds of disaster (shikja: 息災) by reciting Buddha's names and teachings in the esoteric holy words" [*The Encyclopedia of Buddhology*, ibid., p.919].

- to improve goodness and virtue;[92]
- to command everything;[93]
- and to win in praise and philanthropy.[94]

Following these can lead all people to being happy and becoming a buddha. This means people can become a buddha without waiting for billions of years to be a buddha, being just called 'To become a buddha.'

---

91 It (jakiseoungchal: 自己成佛) means one leads to the paths of becoming Buddhahood.

92 It is written as *paustika* in Sanskrit which means "one of the practice theories in order to get happiness and virtue (jeoungik: 增益)" [*The Encyclopedia of Buddhology,* ibid., p.1472].

93 It is written as *abhicāraka* in Sanskrit which may mean " surrendered by prestige or power (hangbok: 降伏)" [*The Encyclopedia of Buddhology,* ibid., pp.1653-4].

94 It (kyeoungai: 敬愛) means respecting and loving something or someone.

The Oldest Twin Vairocana Stuates in the Great Birojurn

The oldest twin gold and wooden Vairocana Statues in Korea are dedicated in the Great Birojurn at Haeinsa Temple. This 200㎡ Great Birojurn is well equipped with thermal-sensors and an earthquake warning system. In the case of a fire or earthquake the statues would be automatically moved into the basement located 6 meters down and be kept safely.

VII. Buddhist's View on the Theory of Esoteric Holy Words

According to the theory of the esoteric holy words,[95] the *Vairocana* himself as son of a king with a piety about the ignorance of lay living things showed all the procession to becoming the *Sakyamuni*-Buddha by leaving home in spit of a prince and by practicing asceticism. Like the Buddhist's view on the theory of the written holy words,[96] the *Nirmanakāya-Buddha* that transformed from the *Dharma*-Body Buddha helps the laymen see what the *Variocana* is like.

---

95 It is written as milkyo(密敎) in Korean which may mean the theory of esoteric holy words. It is often translated into "school", instead of "the words". Here we take 'words'[*Korean-English Buddhist Dictionary with Sanskrit and English Equivalents* op cit, p.161].

96 "It is the written holy words of Buddhism (hyunkyo: 現敎) like the Bible" [*The Encyclopedia of Buddhology,* ibid., p.1673].

The *Nirmanakāya* came at first from the *Variocana* followed by the *Sambhokāya*. Since the view on the 3 embodied Buddhas[97] by the esoteric holy words become that of four Buddhas[98] according to the written holy

---

97 "It is the view on 3 Embodiment Buddha Bodies: the *Dharmakāya-Buddha*, the *Sambhokāya*, and the *Nirmanakāya*(samshinkweon: 三身觀)" 〔*The Encyclopedia of Buddhology,* ibid., pp.751-2〕. The *Trikaya* doctrine (Sanskrit, literally "Three bodies"; samshin(三身) Chinese: *Sānshēn*, Japanese: sanjin) is an important Buddhist teaching both on the nature of reality, and the nature of a Buddha. By the 4th century the *Trikāya* Doctrine had assumed the form that we now know. Briefly, the doctrine says that a Buddha has three *kāyas* or *bodies*: the nirmanakāya or *created body* which manifests in time and space; the sambhogakāya or *body of mutual enjoyment* which is a body of bliss or clear light manifestation; and the *Dharmakāya* or *Truth body* which embodies the very principle of enlightenment and knows no limits or boundaries 〔Internet (2010) Available: http://en.wikipedia.org/wiki/Nirmanakaya〕.

98 "It is the view on 4 Embodiment Buddha Bodies: the Variocana(the *Dharmakāya-Buddha*), the *Sambhogakāya,* the *Nirmanakāya* and the *Shakyamuni*(sashinkweon: 四身觀)" 〔*The Encyclopedia of Buddhology,* ibid., p.673〕. The Vajrayana sometimes refers to a fourth body, called the Svabhavikakāya (Wylie: ngo bo nyid kyi

words. From the *Buddhakāya* of the written and esoteric holy words, the four Buddhas in the esoteric holy words become the *Variocana,* while the view of 3 Buddhas in the written holy words becomes the *Sambhogakāya*.[99]

The enlightened Buddhist[100] becomes the *Dharmakāya*;

sku, THDL: ngo wo nyi kyi ku), meaning essential body [Internet (2010) Available: http://en.wikipedia.org/wiki/Nirmanakaya].

[99] "It is called 3 kinds of Buddhas: the *Dharmakāya-Buddha*, the *Sambhokāya*, and the *Nirmanakaya*(bupboyeungwha: 法報應化)" [*The Encyclopedia of Buddhology,* ibid., p.508.]. The *Sambhogakāya* (Sanskrit: "body of enjoyment", Tib: *longs.sku*) is the second mode or aspect of the Trikaya. *Sambhogakāya* has also been translated as the "deity dimension", "body of bliss" or "astral body". *Sambhogakāya* refers to the luminous form of clear light the Buddhist practitioner attains upon the reaching the highest dimensions of practice. Conversely, it is also considered one of the primary means by which the Dharmakaya is made manifest. Consequently, the *Sambhogakaya* encompasses "celestial" Buddhas such as Bhaisajyaguru, etc., as well as advanced bodhisattvas such as Avalokitesvara and Manjusri [Internet (2010) Available: http://en.wikipedia.org/wiki/Sambhogak %C4%81ya].

[100] "One of the 3 kinds of Buddha Bodies: the *Dharmakāya-Buddha*, the *Sambhokāya*, and the *Nirmanakāya* (jasungshin: 自性身)" [*The*

the Accepted Body of the *Vairocana*[101] becomes the *Sambhogakāya*; the Changed Body of the *Vairocana* becomes the *Nirmanakāya*; and the Transformed Body of the *Vairocana*[102] also becomes the *Nirmanakāya*.

Encyclopedia of Buddhology, ibid., p.1345].

[101] "One of the 3 kinds of Buddha Bodies: the *Dharmakāya-Buddha*, the *Sambhokāya*, and the *Nirmanakāya* (suyounshin: 受用身)" 〔*The Encyclopedia of Buddhology,* ibid., p.888〕.

[102] "One of the 4 kinds of Buddha Bodies(dunglyushin: 等流身): the Vairocana, the *Dharmakāya-Buddha*, the *Sambhokāya* (dunglyushin: 等流身), and the *Nirmanakāya*" 〔*The Encyclopedia of Buddhology,* ibid., p.333〕.

VIII. The Substance, Characteristics, and Function of the *Dharmakāya-Buddha*

The Chaesangyoung[103] (substance, characteristics, and function of the *Dharmakāya-Buddha* as the theory of Yukdaesamansammil:[104] the 6 unimpeded interrelated meta-elements of humanity and universe and 3 secret actions)[105]

---

103 This paper takes the term as substance, characteristics, and function (chesangyoung; 體相用)." According to arising Buddha theory, there are 3 kinds of elements: substance, characteristics, and function" [*The Encyclopedia of Buddhology, op cit.*, p.1545]. However, someone explains it as Essence-Function (體用), a key concept in East Asian Buddhism and particularly that of Korean Buddhism, was refined in the syncretic philosophy and worldview of Wonhyo [Internet (2010) Available: http://en.wikipedia.org/wiki/Won-Yo].

104 It is written as lukdaiesamanammil(六大四曼三密) in Korean. See lukdai(六大) in [*The Encyclopedia of Buddhology.* ibid., p.1195], and lukdaimuahi(六大無碍) in [ibid., p.1195], and saman(四蔓) in [ibid., p.652].

is the *Dharma* that explains everything as well as the active *sūtra*.[106]

As the unanimated truth appears both with the cycling laws of cause and effect and with the activity of the 4 wisdoms and 4 powers,[107] so the laymen get to be aware of Buddhahood[108] in their actual life.

Living/Life is the result of transmission by practice and virtue.[109] We should diligently practice the 3 secret

---

105 "It can be summarized such as 6 boundless interrelated meta-elements of humanity and universe: land, water, fire, wind, emptiness and its consciousness; (p.1195.) which has 3 secret activities and effects of body, speech and mind.(lukdaisammil: 六大三密)" 〔*The Encyclopedia of Buddhology.* ibid., pp.733-4〕.

106 It is written as kyungjun(經典: *sūtra*) in Korean.

107 There are "4 kinds of wisdom in Pubsanjong(法相宗) (p.702) and 4 kinds of power: believing, practising, energy, and wisdom (sajisaryek: 四智四力)"〔*The Encyclopedia of Buddhology,* ibid., p.647〕.

108 It is written as buddhahood in Sanskrit which means "becoming a buddha(gak: 覺)"〔*The Encyclopedia of Buddhology,* ibid., pp.13-4〕.

activities and charity/alms[110] to accomplish our virtue and wisdom (*upasampanna*).[111] It is necessary for us to practice the meta-event-and-principle truth in both man-made event and Buddha world truth.[112] We should find out the reasons for the things we have experienced and judge their value.

The 3 secret activities[113] are our choice because every activity has its start and end which are always related

---

[109] "In order to become a Buddha, layman needs good deeds, wisdom(bokji: 福智: p.561), and transferred knowledge from others(jeonshoo: 傳受)" 〔*The Encyclopedia of Buddhology*, ibid., p.1382〕.

[110] It (hisa: 喜捨) is a kind of alms in Buddhism.

[111] It means "all kinds of good deeds and pleasure and happiness from the deeds and wisdom (bokduckjihye: 福德智慧)" 〔*The Encyclopedia of Buddhology*, ibid., p.559〕.

[112] "There should be established as the meaning of both the moral in the Buddha world and the real aspect in the mundane world(saripilgu: 事理必具)" 〔*The Encyclopedia of Buddhology*, ibid., p.125〕.

[113] It (sameunshangwhal: 三隱生活) refers to the three secret actions of body, speech and mind in Buddhism.

to the personal or public interest, resulting in good or evil/bad outcomes.

The results of our lives are the inward proof[114] of one's personal actions. Everything that a person has done reflects profits or losses and personal or public interests, which can lead to self-awakening[115] by the dependence of cause and effect.

If one practices this activity, every wish will be accomplished and be concreted such as virtue, wisdom, and light, which purifies this mundane life.

---

114 It (naijueong: 內證) refers to the inner awakening experience in Buddhism〔*The Encyclopedia of Buddhology,* p.219〕.
115 "Thanks to right wisdom, one gets to the truth of Buddha(jeoungduk: 證得)"〔*The Encyclopedia of Buddhology,* ibid., p.1470〕.

IX. The *Dharmakāya-Buddha* as Present Body and Mind[116]

Every fact that appears in all directions, places, spaces, or three cycles of time[117] and everything good or bad

---

116 It may mean "Dharma*kāya-Buddha* in itself" (dangchebubmoon: 當體法門). The **Dhammakāya** is a Pāli word meaning" the present body of *Dharma*" or the body of **enlightenment**. It can refer to: Wat Phra Dhammakāya, a Thai Buddhist temple; The *Dhammakāya Movement* and the *Dhammakāya* Foundation, which originated at that temple; The Mahayana Buddhist concept of *Dharma* body; note that this is normally referred to by the similar Sanskrit term *Dharmakāya*, because Pāli is rarely used to discuss Mahayana Buddhism, *Dhammakāya* Meditation, a meditation technique [Internet (2010) Available: http://en.wikipedia.org/wiki/Dhammakaya].

117 By the Buddhists it may be read as "sibansamse(十方三世) in Korea, which means every direction and endless space, referring to as "Buddha's 10 direction world and three periods: past, present and future."

that I have experienced are the *Dharma* through the act of the *Dharmakāya-Buddha* in himself (the present body and mind in itself).

With the secret form/color[118] every aspect in itself accords with Buddhism teachings. Every experience in itself is just the *Dharma* and the fact is just the *sūtra*.

The written holy words can be read with literacy knowledge while the esoteric holy words as body, spoken, and awakening language (the esoteric holy words of three secrets) can be understood without any literacy knowledge.

Buddhists who only study the esoteric holy words on the *karma* of body, speech, and mind can understand this *Dharma*. According to each one's surroundings in which there is no distinction between literacy and illiteracy it is possible to distinguish the good path from the bad one. Who else should take the bad path, instead

---

118 It (mileunshaik: 密隱色) refers the secret form and color from body, speech and mind actions.

of the right path?

By distinguishing between good and bad[119] and the cause or the effect,[120] and without taking any pains, we

Main Viarocana Statue in the Daijurkwhangjurn
The Vairocana Statue with honored Buddha Statues is dedicated at Haeinsa Temple. Besides, *81,258 Wooden Boards of Buddha Sûtra* (1237~1248 AD plus 5 years of preparation) was recorded as a World Cultural Heritage by UNESCO in 1995.

---

119 It (sunak: 善惡) means good and bad action in Buddhism [*The Encyclopedia of Buddhology*, op cit., p.828].

120 It (inkwa: 因果) refers to cause and effect dependence [*The Encyclopedia of Buddhology*, ibid., p.1282].

are happily getting on the path to becoming a buddha with the awakening of the unlimited *Dharma* of Buddhism realm in every place, time, and space.[121]

---

[121] It (mujinbubkye: 無盡法界) may be referred to as "the unlimited Dharma realm of every secret aspect and form in Buddhahood." [*The Encyclopedia of Buddhology*, ibid., p.421]

X. The 6 Great Unimpeded Meta-Elements of Humanity and Universe

The 6 great unimpeded meta-elements of humanity and universe without any obstacles or resistance[122] are land, water, fire, wind, emptiness, and the energy consciousness of mind. The above first 5 elements are of a material-nature and the last one is the energy consciousness of mind, which is one's intention.

These 6 great unimpeded meta-elements are composed of human and universal interrelationships with causes (*hetu*)[123] and their dependency (*prataya*).[124] Since the

---

122 "In Endless Buddha World or Pure Land, there are 6 great unimpeded meta-elements of humanity and universe: land, water, fire, wind, emptiness, and the energy of mind consciousness whcih are all free from any obstacles or resistance (lukdaimuyei: 六大無碍)" [*The Encyclopedia of Buddhology*, ibid., p.1195. and see footnote 135 and 136].

principle of Buddhism is a religion where human beings are the center of the universe, being in the center of the interrelationship of causes (*hetu*) and their dependency (*prataya*), all human beings are composed of the 6 great unimpeded meta-elements of humanity and universe with freedom from all obstacles or resistances as follows:

- The land has an awakening character to behold the Buddha-nature within oneself[125] and leads us to becoming a character of land-nature or solidity[126] as

---

123 "The inward causes will bring their results(in: 因)" [*The Encyclopedia of Buddhology,* ibid., p.1280].

124 It is written as *prataya* in Sanskrit which means "the results of certain causes(yeun: 緣)" [*The Encyclopedia of Buddhology,* ibid., p.1062].

125 "Self-awakening is the way to beholding the Buddha-nature within oneself(kyeunsung: 見性)" [*The Encyclopedia of Buddhology,* ibid., p.45]

126 It means "character of land-nature or solidity (jidai: 地大)." There are Four Great Elements: Earth—solidity, Water—fluidity, Fire—eat and Wind—oscillation [Internet(2010) Available: http://en.wikipedia.org/wiki/Outline_of_Buddhism].

a fixed form.

- The water as moisture becomes a character of fluidity or water-nature.[127]
- The fire as hot-nature becomes a character of heat.[128]
- The wind as moving-nature becomes a character of motion, action, and its change.[129]
- The emptiness as inexplicable and almighty nature becomes the character of acceptability for oscillation[130] as 4 meta unimpeded things and their circulations.[131]

---

[127] It means "one of the 4 great elements that has water character(sudai: 水大)" 〔*The Encyclopedia of Buddhology*, ibid., p.878〕.

[128] It means "one of the 4 great elements that has fire character(whadai: 火大)" 〔*The Encyclopedia of Buddhology*, ibid., p.1708〕.

[129] It means "one of the 4 great elements that has wind character(pungdai: 風大)" 〔*The Encyclopedia of Buddhology*, ibid., p.1637〕.

[130] It means "one of the 4 great elements that has emptiness character(kongdaie: 空大)" 〔*The Encyclopedia of Buddhology*, ibid., p.87〕.

[131] It means "one of the 4 great elements that has the character of air and freedom(yungtong: 融通). "There is neither confusing nor differentiated(yung: 融) or there is no obstacle/hindrance because of all consciousness (dal: 達)" 〔*The Encyclopedia of*

- The energy consciousness of mind as an awakening nature becomes a characteristic of awakening the 5 other elements as the action or move of mind consciousness.[132]

Even if there is a general cause (*hetu*) and if there isn't an equivalent dependency (*prataya*) to help them without their interrelationship, everything in the world will be difficult to grow and get to succeed.

If someone truly sees the intangible and inexplicable interrelationship of causes (*hetu*) and their dependency (*prataya*) then without any hesitation there is the answer to all things in human life. The Buddha came to know the true aspects of these 6 great unimpeded meta-elements of humanity and universe.

Buddhology, ibid., p.1221].

[132] It means "great mind conscious action for awaking(sikdai: 識大)" [*The Encyclopedia of Buddhology*. ibid., pp.916-7].

XI. Becoming a Buddha Rapidly by Three Mystic Meta-Elements(Sammilgalgisokgilhyeun)[133]

Every aspect of life is composed of the 6 great unimpeded meta-elements of humanity and universe with the causes (*hetu*) and their dependency (*prataya*) each having an effect in itself. These are named as the 3 mystic meta-elements of body, speech, and mind.[134]

As Buddhism in general originated from a human religion, every effect and cause in the universe is compared with everyday life (composed of body, speech

---

133 All lay living things are quickly able to become a buddha with the three great meta-elements: Buddha's grace; the secret actions of body, speech and mind; and their attribute (sammilgalgisok-gilhyeun: 三密加持速疾顯)" 〔*The Encyclopedia of Buddhology*, ibid., pp.733-4〕.

134 There are "3 secret karmas of body, speech and mind(sammil: 三密)" 〔*The Encyclopedia of Buddhology*, ibid., pp.733-4〕.

and mind). In the written holy words everyday life is called the 3 mystic works (three *karmas*,[135] which means the works from body, speech, and mind),[136] while in the esoteric holy words the 3 mystic works from body, speech and mind are called the 3 actions of body, speech and mind,[137] and their interrelated causes and effects lead us to becoming a buddha. In the written holy words, the basic way is to wander with an unclear mind,[138] while in the esoteric holy words it is being clearly able to see what it truly is.

At the place of purifying the mystic works from body,

---

[135] It (<u>samyeup</u>: 三業) means 3 karmas from or by the actions of body, speech, and mind in Buddhism.

[136] It is written as *trīni karmāni* in Sanskrit which means "the karma from or by body, speech and mind" [*The Encyclopedia of Buddhology,* ibid., p.758].

[137] It (<u>sammilhyeoung</u>: 三密行) refers to the 3 mystic actions form body, speech and mind in Buddhism [*The Encyclopedia of Buddhology,* ibid., p.734].

[138] It means "wandering with unclear mind like a drunken person(<u>mihok</u>: 迷惑)" [*The Encyclopedia of Buddhology,* ibid., p.439].

speech and mind (three *karmas*) there are 3 mystic actions from body, speech and mind. There can be nothing purified without Buddha's grace on lay living things,[139] our good practices[140] with the power of virtue and goodness,[141] and the united power of the Land of Buddha's *Dharma*.

The power of virtue and goodness can be practiced by the mystic actions from body, speech and mind as follows:

- practicing the theory of Buddha's teachings/meta-principle truth as the belief of the lay disciple[142] is

---

139 It means "the Buddha's virtue and good deeds for the lay living things(kajiryek: 加持力)" 〔*The Encyclopedia of Buddhology*, ibid., pp.10-1〕.

140 The person practices asceticism and Buddha Truth by himself (kwanhaingja: 觀行者)" 〔*The Encyclopedia of Buddhology*, ibid., p.111〕.

141 "The power can have good results from doing good deeds(kongduckryek: 功德力) or by two kinds of the power: religious one, and lay living things' one" 〔*The Encyclopedia of Buddhology*, ibid., p.87〕.

the mystic action from body,[143]
- speaking the theory of Buddha's teachings/meta-principle truth as the belief of the lay disciple is the mystic action from speech,[144]
- and possessing the theory of Buddha's teachings/meta-principle truth as the belief of the lay disciple is the mystic action from mind.[145]

Since the 3 mystic actions of body, speech and mind are the way of becoming a buddha, one will become

---

142 The theory(buliseul: 佛이說) can't be explained by lay people's truth, but can be separated by the meta truth of the Buddha in Buddhism.

143 "It is one of the three secrets: the secret action of body(sinmil: 身密) which can be explained by attitude or appearance" [*The Encyclopedia of Buddhology*, ibid., p.923].

144 "It is one of the three secrets: the secret action of speech(kumil: 口密) which can be explained by language activity or speech" [*The Encyclopedia of Buddhology*, ibid., p.134].

145 "It is one of the three secrets: the secret action of mind(yeimil: 意密) which can be referred to as the every mental/conscious activity in the universe" [*The Encyclopedia of Buddhology*, ibid., p.1231].

a buddha very soon as the result of these good actions.

Everyone has 3 mystic actions from body, speech and mind[146] and even livestock and poor-hungry ghosts in hell (*tiryagyoni-loka*)[147] have such actions.

---

146 It means "the 3 secret actions of body, speech and mind (sammilhyengwe: 三密行爲)" 〔*The Encyclopedia of Buddhology*, ibid., p.734〕.

147 "Livestock may be referred to as ***tiryagyoni***(畜生餓鬼) in Sanskrit" 〔*The Encyclopedia of Buddhology*, p.1559〕. "The ghost in the hell may be referred to as preta in Sanskrit, which is born from the bad deeds of previous world" 〔*The Encyclopedia of Buddhology*, ibid., p.993〕. **Tiryagyoni-loka** or *Tiracchāna-yoni* (Tib: *dud 'gro*) —This world comprises all members of the animal kingdom that are capable of feeling suffering from the smallest insect to the elephant. Internet (2010) Available: http://en.wikipedia.org/wiki/Buddhist_cosmology. *Preta*, (Sanskrit) or *Peta* (Pāli) is the name for a type of (arguably supernatural) being described in Buddhist, Hindu, Sikh, and Jain texts that undergoes more than human suffering, particularly an extreme degree of hunger and thirst. They are often translated into English as "hungry ghosts" from the Chinese, which in turn is derived from later Indian sources generally followed in Mahayana Buddhism 〔Internet (2010) Available: http://en.wikipedia.org/wiki/Preta〕.

If the *Dharma* of this land (*dharma-dhātu*) is purified, every living thing becomes a buddha. Since everything in this land is interrelated, the infinite jewel country[148] that is attached to the Emperor of Jasuk (a guardian Buddha God: *Indra-rāja*)[149] represents each other. The country is composed of the jewels in tight knit nets[150] forming a beautiful scene.[151] As everything in the world can be composed by the help of each other, it becomes a grand pure land of Buddhism[152] which is the Pure Realm

---

148 "There are 4 masters in the jewel country(mushubojoo: 無數寶珠) in which there are all kinds of jewel from the southeast area of Snow mountain" [*The Encyclopedia of Buddhology*, ibid., p.553].

149 "It is referred to as *Indra-rāja* in Sanskrit(jesukchungwang: 帝釋天王" [*The Encyclopedia of Buddhology*, ibid., p.1420].

150 "The jewels that are in the tight knit nets shine beautiful lights, commanding marvelous scene(jungjungjeimang: 重重帝網)" [*The Encyclopedia of Buddhology*, ibid., p.1415].

151 It may be referred to as "a very beautiful scene(ildaimikwan: 一大美觀)."

152 It may mean as "decorating body, land or residence with beautiful things. There are 29 pure lands of Buddha(莊嚴世界)" [*The Encyclopedia of Buddhology*, ibid., p.1363].

of Buddhism.[153]

Pubsungsa Temple

Located on Mt. Youngshuk in Changyoungcounty, the temple was founded in 1996 by Duckodang Pubsung (1928-2005). She dedicated the engraved stone Vairocana Statue in the Daekwangmaeyingjurn.

---

153 "It is Buddha's Land in which Buddha teaches for saving lay living things(bulgukjeungto: 佛國淨土)" 〔*The Encyclopedia of Buddhology*, ibid., p.591〕.

XII. The *Sabhava Dharmakāya*[154]

Now, let us understand the *Vairocana* who exists in our minds representing oneness as 3 celestial realms of Buddhism and being universal.

If we see a tree in the garden every day, we are not usually aware of its growth, so the improvement in Buddha-character cannot be seen through the eyes of those who see it every day. Being aware of this principle in advance and with regular and good practice we can just see it in 5 or 6 years; while believing in Buddhism and helping each other consistently within the family.

---

154 "It (jasungbupshin: 自性法身) is one of the 3 bodies as a natural true body: law(bup: 法), reward(bo: 報), and arhat(eung: 應)" [*The Encyclopedia of Buddhology*, ibid., p.1345].

XIII. The Written Holy Words and the Esoteric Holy Words

In Buddhism there are 2 kinds of holy words: written and esoteric holy words. The written holy words are *Sakyamuni's* teachings in writing, while the esoteric holy words are the most profound and deepest truth in Buddhism, which is mystic truth that Buddhists can only see by understanding and reaching a certain level of Buddha's truth. Furthermore, the esoteric holy words contain several theories and principles such as:

- Sun-ism *(dhyāna-*ism),[155]
- Mita-ism(*Amitabha* Buddha),[156]

---

155 "This is one ideology for practicing Buddhism(sunshashang: 禪思想) which always pays the mindful attention to one thing and thinks of it entirely and completely" [*The Encyclopedia of Buddhology*, ibid., pp.817-9].

156 It is abridged name from "*Amitabha* Buddha(彌陀思想), which is written as *Amitābha Buddha* in Sanskrit that is one of the Buddhas"

- Gwahsehum-ism (*Buddhisattva* of Compassion),[157]
- Miruk-ism(*Maitreya*),[158] and so on.

All of them have been developed as a united Buddhism. It is the best *Dharma* in Buddhism which explains universal rules like a way of getting actual benefit, as well as reaching the realms of Buddhism Land after death.

In the past, the esoteric holy words that came from Great Monk of Hyetong (665?)[159] in the Silla Dynasty[160]

[*The Encyclopedia of Buddhology,* ibid., p.1004].

[157] It is "one of 16 views on the Buddha land and Buddha body(kwaneunsashang: 觀音思想)" [*The Encyclopedia of Buddhology,* p.107. and *Guide to Korean Buddhist Temples,* op cit., p.93].

[158] It was "one religious theory in old China that respected Miruk Buddha(彌勒佛: future Buddha) which would appear in the future(amisashang: 彌勒思想)" [*The Encyclopedia of Buddhology, op cit.,* p.433].

[159] "He was one of the great monks(Hyetong: 惠通) in Silla Dynasty" [*The Encyclopedia of Buddhology,* ibid., p.1695]

[160] The Old Korean Dynasty(BC 57~935 AD).

were distributed from the royal family (palace) to the popular laymen. Though it flourished until the Koryo Dynasty,[161] it was merged with other religions by the restraining policy against Buddhism[162] in the Chosun Dynasty.[163] Thus, all kinds of the esoteric holy words and historical records for national events[164] were completely destroyed.

In the theory of the written holy words, it is an assertion of Simbonsaekmal[165] (a principle that mind rises first and

---

161 The Middle Korean Dynasty(818~1392 AD).
162 It (yeukbuljungchak: 抑佛政策) was one of the policies in the Late Korean Dynasty(Choshun: 朝鮮). "The deep Buddhist influence on the previous dynasty led the leaders to urging the king to uproot Buddhist economic and political influence, which led to exile in the mountains for monks and their disciples" [Internet (2010) Available: http://www.lonelyplanet.com/south-korea/history].
163 The Late Korean Dynasty(1395~1926 AD).
164 It (yeagueak: 儀軌) refers to the old historical books and recording [*The Encyclopedia of Buddhology*. ibid., pp.1229-30].
165 It (shimbonsaekmal: 心本色末) means "Mind becomes first and gets the form later in Buddhism."

form/aspect appears later). Our mind comes from its basic source or energy and ends at the form/aspect. Someone's mind is oriented on the future of Buddhism, and in the long run becomes the after-death theory[166] of Buddhism.

Shimbonsaekmal in the written holy words, however, means that the actual form/aspect and principle in the written holy words are so delicate and fundamental that they should come first. Instead, the form/actual aspect and things that are empty in the end should come next or after. The religious theory of the written holy words is a unitary principle theory in which everything comes from one principle.

Saekshimbuli (mind and form/aspect is not separated into two elements)[167] in the esoteric holy words whose assertion/principle is that the form/aspect and mind are not different each other. In the long run, it has become

---

[166] It (sahoo: 死後) means afterdeath of all the human beings.

[167] "Form may be referred to as materials while mind may be referred to as spirit. Thus, two words are the same one, not dual (saekshimbuli: 色心不異)" [*The Encyclopedia of Buddhology*, ibid., p.800].

the practical Buddhism for the present way of life.

The meaning of <u>saekshimbuli</u> in the esoteric holy words is that not only are all things just truth, but they don't contain a form/aspect by appearance becoming just one principle. Things and mind have equality as everything in the world in accordance with Buddhism *Dharma*/teachings, which means the teachings in the esoteric holy words have two principle theories.

The *Dharmakāya-Buddha* as a founder of the esoteric holy words always saves lay living things by the way of true principles while the *Nirmanakāya-Buddha* as a founder of the written holy words always saves all laymen by using instruments or methods such as books.

The *Dharmakāya-Buddha* that cannot teach using these instruments becomes the *Nirmanakāya-Buddha* according to the proper time and principle. Thus, the *Nirmanakāya-Buddha* appears as Buddha in this world to use instruments to teach. If He wants to use the way of true principle, He should become the *Dharmakāya-Buddha* again.

XIV. The Theory of the Written Holy Words and the Esoteric Holy Words as One Buddhism

The written and esoteric holy words are one Buddhism, but their start and end[168] are different. When can we see Buddha Bliss Land/Paradise before death if we are still wandering here and there?

Since this and that religion comes from one principle by different instruments there will be no success if we open this or that door of religion.

Though brown and red beans are the same plant with their different names, what is the real property if they are mixed in one dish?

Since you and I are the same person with different wills, let's preach to laymen according to our will without any hesitation of coming or going.

---

168 It (jongji: 宗旨) means conclusion or results in Buddhism.

Though the *Dharmakāya* and the *Nirmanakāya* is one Buddha, it doesn't have the same name.

When we arrive at the perfect states of purification, sufficient virtue (*suddha*), and satisfaction,[169] we get to take the position of all laymen's *Nariva* (*mahāyāna*).[170] Things and mind come from the same body, but there are two kinds of sexual appearance: man and woman in it. Building our willingness[171] or main ideas is helping

---

169 "There are 18 kinds of virtue and good deeds which are full of Buddha land(<u>wonman</u>: 圓滿)" [*The Encyclopedia of Buddhology,* ibid., p.1160].

170 "It is Dharma that gets the lay living things to reach the state of awakening-one(<u>daiseung</u>: 大乘)" [*The Encyclopedia of Buddhology,* p.274.]. **Mahayana**, lit. "great vehicle", A major branch of Buddhism practiced in China, Tibet, Japan, Korea, Vietnam, and Taiwan. Main goal is to achieve buddhahood or samyaksambuddha [Internet (2010) Available: http://en.wikipedia.org/wiki/Mahayana].

171 It may mean "the land for the seed of 8 kinds of consciousness and awareness(<u>jongji</u>: 宗旨), which can affect the energy of discovering all kinds of aspects or ideas of the material mind(<u>mulshim</u>: 物心)" [*The Encyclopedia of Buddhology,* ibid.,

us to become a new buddha.

Stone Vairocana Statue in the Birojurn

The Vairocana Statue at Bulgoksa Temple in Changwon City was appointed as Korean national treasure no. 436 in 1966. This is one of the typical Vairocana Statues(from 850-900AD) created during the Unified Silla Dynasty and is very similar to the Vairocana Statue at Dongwhasa Temple in Daegu City.

p.219].

XV. The *Variocana* Shown in the *Avatamsaka Sūtraism* (Whaom *Sūtra*. Whaomism in Korean)[172]

---

172 The *Avatamsaka Sūtra* (華嚴經) was written in stages, beginning from at least 500 years after the death of the Buddha. It is "a very long text composed of a number of originally independent scriptures of diverse provenance, all of which were combined, probably in Central Asia, in the late third or the fourth century CE." Two full Chinese translations of the *Avatamsaka Sūtra* were made. Fragmentary translation probably began in the 2nd century CE, and the famous *Ten Stages Sūtra,* often treated as an individual scripture, was first translated in the 3rd century. The first complete Chinese version was completed by Buddhabhadra around 420, and the second by Śikṣānanda around 699. There is also a translation of the *Gandavyuha* by Prajñā around 798. The second translation includes more sutras than the first, and the Tibetan translation, which is still later, includes even more. Scholars conclude that sūtras were being added to the collection [Internet(2010) Available: http://en.wikipedia.org/wiki/%C5%9Aik%E1%B9%A3%C4%81nanda]. '*Sūtra*'(kyeungjun: 經典) may refer to: *Sūtra* – A type of literary composition in Buddhism or Hinduism(佛經典). "In Buddhism, the *sūtra* refers mostly to canonical scriptures, many of which are regarded as records of the oral teachings of Gautama Buddha. In Chinese, these are known as 經 (pinyin: *jīng*). These teachings are assembled in

Avatamsaka Sūtraism is one theory established on the *Avantamsaka Sūtra*, which is called the main *sūtra*. Its philosophical structure is related to the original dependence of Buddhism realms (*Buddha-avatamsaka-mahāvaipulya-sūtra*).[173]

Nothing alone stands or occurs in the universe. Everything has certain causes on each other at a certain time and space. Everything transcends each other; and fuses into one as follows:

---

part of the Tripitaka which is called Sutra Pitaka. There are also some Buddhist texts, such as the Platform Sūtra. That are called sūtras despite being attributed to much later authors" [Internet (2010) Available: http://en.wikipedia.org/wiki/S%C5%ABtra]. "Whaomism and *Whaom Sutras*: whaomsasang(華嚴思想) and whaomkyung(華嚴經)" in Korean [Internet (2010) Available: http://ref.daum.net/item/11415305].

[173] This (bupkyeyenkye: 法界緣起) is "a theory that is viewed as one great original dependence of the universe in itself based on the main philosophical background of *Avantamsake Sūtra*. It is written as "*Buddha-avatamsaka-mahāvaipulya-sūtra*" in Sanskrit [*The Encyclopedia of Buddhology*, pp.501-2].

- the unimpeded infinite cause and effect interrelationship principle as the meta-event truth of mundane world,[174]
- 10 features of infinitely actual cause and effect original dependences,[175]
- each seed/aspect fused without any hindrance/obstacle,[176]
- and the roles of 6 great unimpeded meta-elements that have harmonious characteristics or aspects and their independence in the universe[177] and so on,

---

174 This means "the original independences between the particular objects and non-particular ones(yimuyijinyeunki: 異無異塵緣起)" [*The Encyclopedia of Buddhology,* p.1247].

175 It may be read as "shiphyenmoon(十玄門)" or "shiphyenyeankimuyepubmoon (十玄緣起無礙法門)" in Korean [*The Encyclopedia of Buddhology,* ibid., p.989].

176 "Each seed/aspect can be fused without any hindrance/obstacle (luksangwonyoung: 六相圓融 or sangipsangjuk: 相入相卽). There are 6 characteristics/aspects: whole and parts, unity and diversity, entirety and its fractions" [*The Encyclopedia of Buddhology,* ibid., p.793].

177 It (shiphyenmoon)(十玄門)" or "shiphyenyeankimuyepubmoon (十玄緣起無礙法門) means "one of Whaom *Sūtra* theories in which

which is the original independence principle between the particular objects and non-particular ones[178] of the *Avantamsake Sūtra*.

Furthermore, the gist (core) of *Avatamsaka Sūtraism* (Whaomism) explains the interrelationship Buddha principle such as:

- the unimpeded infinite cause and effect interrelationship (the original dependence of no differentiated causes and effects) in the meta-event truth of mundane world (the universal truth of the *Avantamsake Sūtra*),[179]
- 10 features of infinitely actual cause and effect original dependences,

---

6 seeds/aspects affect each other to be merged into oneness" [*The Encyclopedia of Buddhology*, ibid., pp.1200-1].

178 It (mujinyeunki: 無盡緣起) means one of the 4 originality dependences [*The Encyclopedia of Buddhology*, p.421].

179 It means "one of the 4 realms of Buddha land which can be referred to as differentiated phenomenal world. Work/business(sa: 事) can be the aspect of objects and the world(kye: 界) can mean as differentiated thing, scope, degree, class, etc(sabupkye: 事法界)" [*The Encyclopedia of Buddhology*, ibid., pp.581-2].

- the roles of 6 great unimpeded meta-elements which have harmonious characteristics or aspects and their independence in the universe,
- mutual entry and good harmony with each other without any difficulties, and so on.

The 4 celestial realms of Buddhism[180] are correlated with both the aspect and the body which are divided into as follows:

- the unimpeded meta-event truth of mundane realm/world (event in the humane or phenomenal world),
- the unimpeded meta-principle truth of Buddhism Land (principle in Buddha-nature),
- all unimpeded meta-truth of both Buddhism Land and mundane world where there are no obstacles (unimpeded meta-principle truth and meta-event truth in both: mundane and phenomenal truths are interdependent),[181]

---

180 It (sabupkye: 四法界) refers to Buddha's 4 realms [*The Encyclopedia of Buddhology.* ibid., pp.659-60].

181 "This is one of the 4 realms of Buddhism and religious principle of Whaom Sūtra. Aspect world and main body world can be fused without any hindrances/obstacle in Buddha land(yisamuai-

- and the unimpeded met-event truth of mundane world where there are no obstacles[182] (phenomena are also interdependent).

The unimpeded meta-event truth world in mundane world represents everything that has its own limitation, compatibility, and differentiated aspect. In the unimpeded meta-principle truth in Buddhism land, not in mundane world,[183] everything always has the same features. However, its aspect and body always keep equality because they cannot separate from each other. This represents the boundless interrelationships of the unimpeded meta-truth world in both Buddhism realm and mundane world.[184] Furthermore, the aspect in itself

---

bupkye: 理事無碍法界)" 〔*The Encyclopedia of Buddhology*, ibid., p.1251〕.

182 "This is one of the 4 realms of Buddhism and religious view of *Whaom Sūtra* Theory. Aspect world and main body world can be fused without any obstacles in lay living things' world(sasamuaibupkye: 事事無碍法界)" 〔*The Encyclopedia of Buddhology*, ibid., p.665〕.

183 It (yibupkye: 理法界) refers to meta-principle *Dharma* realm in Buddhism 〔*The Encyclopedia of Buddhology*, ibid., p.1249〕.

has its cause that keeps fusing, which is called the interrelationships of the unimpeded meta-event truth of the mundane world. It represents the characteristics of *Avatamsaka Sūtraism* (Whaomism) which are generally called the original dependence between the Buddhism celestial realms. Among the infinite correlations[185] whose aspects/forms are explained as 10 features, called those of cause and effect original dependence *Dharma*.

The Lotus Land of Buddhism[186] that is explained in the *Avantamsake Sūtra* can be a big entity which remains confused and develops itself endlessly where there is the compatibility between aspects of land and its body. In this lotus land, the *Vairocana* as the central Buddha

---

184 Refer to footnote no. 182 (Yisamuaibupkye: 理事無碍法界) 〔*The Encyclopedia of Buddhology*. ibid., p.1251〕.

185 "This is one of the religious terms in *Avantamsake Sūtra* (jungjungmujin: 重重無盡). As one can contain the 10, so can the 10 one, which means everything in the universe can be merged into oneness" 〔*The Encyclopedia of Buddhology*, ibid., p.1465〕.

186 It (Yeunwhajangshekye: 蓮華藏世界) is Buddha's Bliss Land 〔*The Encyclopedia of Buddhology*. ibid., pp.1070-1〕.

of the *Avantamsake Sūtra* always shines infinite great light, creating harmony.

The *Vairocana*, as the founder of the *Avantamsake Sūtra* and the *Dharmakāya-Buddha* and the real Body(*kāya*)-Buddha in all the Buddhas, is the real Buddha statue in the universe which common laymen never see with their eyes. Though the Buddha is called Buddha Body of the God, He is neither a common body nor a formed/colorful body, which means every body originated from this inherent Buddha Body.

However, when He is configured as the Buddha, He takes his lotus pedestal, Buddha's sitting style (Buddha's sitting form),[187] with left hand put on the knee and right hand raised gently on the platform decorated with one thousand lotus petals. Each of the 1,000 flower petals around the flower stand of the Buddha Statue is to express millions of nations and lands where all the infinite virtues

---

187 "This is Buddha's sitting position which every monk or Buddha practicer usually takes to get an awareness-one(kyelgabujowa: 結跏趺坐)" 〔*The Encyclopedia of Buddhology*, ibid., p.49〕.

and good deeds[188] and the enormous grandness of imponderable creation is represented and modeled in the Buddhism Pure Land.

The center of the big lotus contains everything in this universe. This lotus world full of purification and light, the ideal Buddha land is called lotus land of Buddhism[189] (the land of the *Vairocana*) or the world of the enormous and grand lotus sea and land of Buddhism (one of the 3 lotus realms/worlds which is compared to the endless and grand sea).[190] This land is called the Buddhism World of Lotus, where there is a big lotus whose center contains every land and thing.

Though there are different expatiations on this world in the *Avantamsake Sūtra* and Peummang *Sūtra* (*Brahmajāla sūtra*[191] one of the Buddha *Sūtras*), both

---

188 These (konduckmuryang: 功德無量) can bring us good results from the good deeds or virtues.

189 It (Whaomsekye: 華嚴世界) means the world of *Avatamsaka Sūtraism*. See [Footnote 49].

190 It is abridged as "yeunwhajangjangemsegye(蓮華藏莊嚴世界海) in Korean" [*The Encyclopedia of Buddhology*, ibid., p.1715].

theories are currently adopted in Korean Buddhism. The ideal world in the *Avantamsake Sūtra* is the same world by the wish and practice of the *Vairocana*. Namely, there is an air windy wheel stratum (the region of the meta-wind-circle)[192] at the bottom of this world and over it there is the scented ocean (the sea surrounding Mt. Sumi).[193] In the scented sea there is a bunch of big lotus

---

191 It is transcribed as *Brahmajāla* in Sanskrit which means "one of the Buddha *Sūtra* for Buddha precepts(bumangkyeung: 梵網經)" 〔*The Encyclopedia of Buddhology*, ibid., pp.493-4〕. The **Brahmajala Sūtra** (Chinese: 梵網經; pinyin: *fàn wǎng jīng*, Japanese: *bonmōkyō*), which are also called the *Brahma's Net Sūtra* is a text of the Mahayana Buddhist canon 〔Internet (2010) Available: http://en.wikipedia.org/wiki/Brahmajala_Sūtra_(Mahayana)〕.

192 The wind-circle realm or air wheel stratum in the land (pungryun: 風輪) as one of the 4 wheels is composed of the empty wheel stratum at the bottom, the air wheel stratum lies on the empty wheel stratum, the water wheel stratum lies on the air wheel stratum and iron wheel stratum lies atop" 〔*The Encyclopedia of Buddhology*, ibid., p.1637〕.

193 It means "the scented ocean which surrounds Mt. Sumi (whangshuhyei: 香水海). There are two seas: the sea of lotus land and the sea of Saba(娑婆: sahā)" 〔*The Encyclopedia of Buddhology*, ibid., p.1666〕.

whose inner part land is the lotus land of Buddhism.

In Pummang *Sūtra* (*Brahmajāla*: one of the Buddhism *Sūtras*), there is the *Vairocana* that sits on the lotus pedestal (the venue of all the Buddhas' sitting)[194] decorated with 1,000 petals where a petal contains each land and there are 1,000 *Sakyamuni* Buddha's transfigured from the *Vairocana* in 1,000 lands. And each land has millions of nations.

Each one of the billion nations had *Sakyamuni* Buddha at that time. Though the study of Lotus Buddhism Land flourished with the great increase of Whaom Religious Theory and the development of *Avatamsaka Sūtraism* (Whaomism) in the old Koryo Dynasty (818-1392 AD),[195] the idea of the Buddhism World of Lotus was not expanded to the laymen compared with the idea of Buddhism Bliss Land (which was in other words, *Amitabha*

---

[194] "The place that all Buddhas either sit on or take a position (yeunwhadai: 蓮花臺)" [*The Encyclopedia of Buddhology*, ibid., p.1069].

[195] Old Middle Dynasty in Korea

Buddha) and the reincarnation theory of *Tusita-deva* in the theory of religion[196]. The reason why it was not easy for the laymen to understand Buddhism World of Lotus was related to the theory of original dependence of Buddhism which means the universe is interrelated to the Buddha *Dharma.*

'The Sabok Tale' in 『*The History of the Three*

---

[196] It may refer to To Sol's 3 gates(兜率 三關). 〔Hyunkark, *Compass of the Good* (Seoul: Yeoulrimwon, 2001), pp.168-70〕. It is written as "Tusita-deva in Sanskrit which may be referred to as the fourth sky of 6 celestial realms and 6000 skies(doshoulchunwhang-sangsul: 兜率天往生說)" 〔*The Encyclopedia of Buddhology*, ibid., p.308〕. ***Tus-ita*** (Sanskrit) or ***Tusita*** (Pāli) is one of the six deva-worlds of the Kāmadhātu, located between the Yāma heaven and the Nirmāsarati heaven. Like the other heavens, *Tusita* is said to be reachable through meditation. It is the heaven where the Bodhisattva *Śvetaketu* (Pāli: Setaketu, "White Banner") resided before being reborn on Earth as Gautama, the historical Buddha; it is, likewise, the heaven where the Bodhisattva *Nātha* ("Protector") currently resides, who will later be born as the next Buddha, Maitreya 〔Internet (2010) Available: http://en.wikipedia.org/wiki/Tusita〕.

Kingdoms: *Kokyure, Backje,* and *Sillar*[197]*』*[198] was written, "When Buddhist Monk, Sabok finished his mother's funeral service with a Great Buddhist Monk, Wonhyoh (617-686),[199] he said, 'As in the old days *Sakyamoni* already entered *Nirvana*[200] in the *sālavṛksa* [201](a tree), so he now wants a person to go to Buddhism

---

[197] Silla (新羅: BC 57〜935 AD) (one of the three kingdoms of old Korea, and one of the longest sustained dynasties in Asian history [Internet (2010) Available: http://en.wikipedia.org/wiki/Silla].

[198] This (samkukyusa: 三國遺事) is one of the Korean old history books by Monk Ilryeon(一連) during the Koryo Dynasty.

[199] Wonhyo (元曉大師: 617〜686 CE) was one of the leading thinkers, writers and commentators of the Korean Buddhist tradition. Essence-Function (體用), a key concept in East Asian Buddhism and particularly that of Korean Buddhism, was refined in the syncretic philosophy and worldview of Wonhyo [Internet (2010) Available: http://en.wikipedia.org/wiki/W%C5%8Dnhyo].

[200] *Nirvāna* (yeluban: 涅槃) (Nibbāna)) is a central concept in Indian religions. In sramanic thought, it is the state of being free from suffering (or *dukkha*). In Hindu philosophy, it is the union with the Supreme being through Moksha. The word literally means "blowing out" — referring, in the Buddhist context, to the blowing out of the fires of greed, hatred, and delusion. [Internet (2010) Available: http://en.wikipedia.org/wiki/Nirvana].

World of Lotus like *Sakyamoni'*. After weeding out Ti-plant (a kind of grass) and carrying his mother's body on his back he went into Buddhism World of Lotus."

The founder of Buddhism World of Lotus is the *Vairocana* that controls the entire universe. This symbolized *Vairocana* is everywhere like air. The *Vairocana* that was transfigured into *Sakyamoni* as *Nirmanakāya-Buddha* variably appears according to time, place, and man.

Though the eyes of human beings that are infatuated with delusion cannot see Him, they can see Him without doubt everywhere with one mindfulness and pure thought. Namely, according not only to the laymen's sincere invocation for something and wish for it, but to the men's activities and boundaries, the *Vairocana* appears in good time and at places with several more or less similar faces with proper activities and teachings.

---

201 "It is written as ***sālavrksa*** in Sanskrit which is a tree composing of forest where *Sakyamuni* got awakened(sarassangsu: 紗羅雙樹) [*The Encyclopedia of Buddhology*, op cit., p.646].

The *Vairocana* with several kinds of bodies, names, and ways of life, teaches the laymen's unimpeded meta-event truth without any rest and saves all of them wherever they live.

However, the *Vairocana* in the *Avantamsake Sūtra* consistently keeps silent. As soon as *Sakyamuni* got enlightened under the *bodhi*-tree he became one body of the *Vairocana* and took the teaching position by the rays of the *Vairocana's* infinite light surrounded by a lot of *bodhisattvas* including Bohhyun-bohsal[202] in the enlightened world. In addition, it has one of the big characteristics where we live in this mundane world. The entire world is purified by the *Vairocana*, not just only Buddha's grand world.

Thanks to our conversion and obedience into Him, in this world we worship the *Vairocana* as *Dharmakāya* that reflects the mundane world originated from Buddha's wisdom into our eyes.

---

202 It (bohyunbohsal: 普賢菩薩) is one of Buddha Bohsals in Buddhism [*Guide to Korean Buddhist Temple*. op cit., p.93].

Besides, it is possible to go to the way of *Vairocana's* world through the activity of becoming *bodhisattva* (Buddhist), which means the process of figuration from un-shaped *Vairocana* through social performance. The activity of <u>bohsal</u> as the best way to awakening is in itself the way of going to the *Vairocana*.

Suljengri Eastern Pagoda
3-Story Stone Pagoda(Korean National Treasure No.34 in 1962) in Changyoung is recorded to have been built in the middle of the 8th C. It can fairly be compatible with the 3-story stone pagoda at Bulkuksa Temple(Korean National Treasure No.21).

XVI. *Avatamaka Sūtra* World[203]

Buddha-*kāya*(Buddha Body) always exists throughout the universe. Appearing in front of all lay living things, He who always answers our questions responds all based on our individual originality dependences. This place is just the Bliss Land of Buddhism as well as the awakening place.

A Volume of the *Sūtra*[204]

I have a volume of the *sūtra* which is not written using paper and ink. Though I open and read it, there

---

[203] *Avantamsaka Sūtra* World may be Buddha's Bliss Land where there is only truth Dharma like paradise [Internet(2011) Available: http://www.budreview.com/news/articleView.html?idxno=702].

[204] It (ilkwenkyung: 一券經) can be a Buddha *sūtra* which is not written with paper and ink but can be read and understood without any letters like mind's symbol reading [Internet(2011) Available: http://blog.daum.net/cigong2500/7361176].

are not any letters in it, but it always illuminates with its infinite light.

XVII. The *Vairocana* Statue and His Hall

In Korean we call the temple, Daejurkgwhangjurn,[205] Daekwangmaeyingjurn (which means 'Hall of Eternally Tranquil Light'), Whaomjurn, Bokwhangjurn, or Birojurn, where the *Vairocana* is dedicated in the hall. In the case of naming this jurnkak (Buddha Hall/Temple)[206] the *Vairocana* is dedicated the central position while *Rhoshana*-Buddha and *Sakyamuni* Buddha are to the left and right of the *Vairocana*. When the hall is called Birojurn[207] or Whaomjurn,[208] it is only common for the

---

205 It (Daejekgwangjurn: 大寂光殿) is the hall name of the *Vairocana* who is dedicated in the temple, the Great Eternal Quite Land, where the vastness of the meditation of the Buddha always preaches *Avantamsaka Sūtra to* lay living things. The building is called Daejurkgwhangjurn. Kim, Kiwhong(1978) 『*Sightseeing of the Haein Temple*』 (Seoul: Woojin Sightseeing Cultural Center, 1978), no page].

206 It (junkag: 殿閣) means the hall name of the Buddha or temple in Korea. See [ibid].

Vairocana alone to be dedicated in the hall.

In general, the *Vairocana* in the hall of the temple sits in the Buddha position shown with jikwonin (which literally means the figures of fingers and hands which become both the awakening for the wisdom of Buddha and the stupidity of laymen as oneness).

However, since the end of the Koryo Dynasty (818-1392 AD) there has often appeared a transformed statue of Buddha with jikwonin. Behind the statue there is the main painting showing the image of the *Vairocana*,[209] which is usually described in a scene giving a lesson of the *Avantamsake Sūtra*.

---

207 It (birojurn: 毘盧殿) means the hall name of the Buddha or temple in Korea where the *Vairocana* Statue is dedicated. See [ibid].

208 This (whaomjurn: 華嚴殿) is the hall name of the Buddha or temple in Korea where the *Vairocana* Statue is dedicated. See [ibid].

209 It (hoobool-taenghwah: 後佛幀畵) is the painting drawn behind the Main Buddha Statue [*The Encyclopedia of Buddhology*, op cit., p.1732. and *Guide to Korean Buddhist Temple*, op cit., p.100].

Vairocana Statue in the Whaomjurn

Located on Mt. Duckwoo in Whamyangcounty Yeoungkaksa Temple(876AD) has one gold and copper Vairocana and 4 other Buddha statues with Whaomkyeungbeunsangdo(a painting drawn behind the main Buddha Statue/s) in the Whaomjurn.

*Sincerely thank all the Buddhists for publishing this book, *the Variocana*.

Worshipping with my hands clasped in prayer (*gassho*)

Buddhist Monk, Jongil
& Choonki, Park

References

현각. 『선의 나침반』. 서울: 열림원, 2001.

Hesse, Herman, *Siddhartha*. Translated by Hilda Rosner. 박상은 역주. 서울: 도솔, 1995. Hongbubwon ed. *The Encyclopedia of Buddhology*. Seoul: Hongbub-won, 1994.

International Dharma Instructors Association. *Guide to Korean Buddhist Temples*. Seoul: Jogye Order Publishing, 1995,

Kim, Kiwhong. 『*Sightseeing of the Haein Temple*』. Seoul: Woojin Sightseeing Cultural Center, 1978.

Ko, Young-seop and Hwang Nam-Ju. *Korean-English Buddhist Dictionary with Sanskrit and English Equivalents*. Seoul: Shinasa, 2010.

Jinkakkyujurn (ed). *Hyuein Hang* . Seoul: Taikwangmunwhasa, 1990.

Paraskevopoulos, John. *Call of the Infinite: The Way of Shin Buddhism*. California: Sophia Perennis Publications, 2009.

Sogyal, Rinpoche. *The Tibetan Book of Living and Dying*. Patrick Gaffney and Andrew Harvey eds. New York: Harper Collins, 1994.

Internet(2010) Available: http://edu.jingak.or.kr/view.php?bid=01_01&bno=20&start_num=0&bst=&chksort=1

Internet(2010) Available: http://en.wikipedia.org/w/index.php?title=Special%3ASearch&search=r%C3%BBp%C4%

Internet(2010) Available: http://english.visitkorea.or.kr/enu/SI/SI_EN_3_1_2_4.jsp?gotoPage=&category=&areaCode=35&folderId=&recommCid=803203&cidList=&cid=264261&out_service=

Internet(2010) Available: http://en.wikipedia.org/wiki/Amitabha_Buddha

Internet(2010) Available http://en.wikipedia.org/wiki/Anitya

Internet(2010) Available: http://en.wikipedia.org/wiki/Asceticism

Internet(2010) Available: http://en.wikipedia.org/wiki/Avidy%C4%81

Internet(2010) Available: http://en.wikipedia.org/wiki/Bodhisattva

Internet(2010) Available: http://en.wikipedia.org/wiki/Bodhisattva_vows

Internet(2010) Available: http://en.wikipedia.org/wiki/Bodhi_Tree

Internet(2010) Available: http://en.wikipedia.org/wiki/Brahmajala_Sutra_(Mahayana)

Internet(2010) Available: http://en.wikipedia.org/wiki/Buddha-nature

Internet(2010) Available: http://en.wikipedia.org/wiki/Buddhism

Internet(2010) Available: http://en.wikipedia.org/wiki/Dabotap

Internet(2010) Available: http://en.wikipedia.org/wiki/Dharma

Internet(2010) Available: http://en.wikipedia.org/wiki/Dharmadhatu

Internet(2010) Available: http://en.wikipedia.org/wiki/Dhammakaya

Internet(2010) Available: http://en.wikipedia.org/wiki/Dharmak%C4%81ya.

Internet(2010) Available: http://en.wikipedia.org/wiki/Dukkha

Internet(2010) Available: http://en.wikipedia.org/wiki/Glossary_of_ Buddhism

Internet(2010) Available: http://en.wikipedia.org/wiki/Jambudvipa

Internet(2010) Available: http://en.wikipedia.org/wiki/Mahayana

Internet(2010) Available: http://en.wikipedia.org/wiki/Mindfulness

Internet(2010) Available: http://en.wikipedia.org/wiki/Manju

Internet(2010) Available: http://en.wikipedia.org/wiki/Nirmanakaya

Internet(2010) Available: http://en.wikipedia.org/wiki/Nirvana

Internet(2010) Available: http://en.wikipedia.org/wiki/Outline_of_ Buddhism

Internet(2010) Available: http://en.wikipedia.org/wiki/Preta

Internet(2010) Available: http://en.wikipedia.org/wiki/Pratyeka- Buddha

Internet(2010) Available: http://en.wikipedia.org/wiki/Purity_in_ Buddhism

Internet(2010) Available: http://en.wikipedia.org/wiki/Shurangama_ Samadhi_Sutra

Internet(2010) Available: http://en.wikipedia.org/wiki/Sambhogak% C4%81ya

Internet(2010) Available: http://en.wikipedia.org/wiki/Sambhoga- kaya.

Internet(2010) Available: http://en.wikipedia.org/wiki/Sabh%C4%81

Internet(2010) Available: http://en.wikipedia.org/wiki/%C5%9Aik% E1%B9%A3%C4%81nanda

Internet(2010) Available: http://en.wikipedia.org/wiki/Shurangama_

Samadhi_Sutra

Internet(2010) Available: http://en.wikipedia.org/wiki/Sukh%C4%81vat%C4%AB.

Internet(2010) Available: http://en.wikipedia.org/wiki/Svabh%C4%81va

Internet(2010) Available: http://en.wikipedia.org/wiki/S%C5%ABtra

Internet(2010) Available: http://en.wikipedia.org/wiki/Tusita

Internet(2010) Available: http://en.wikipedia.org/wiki/Vairocana.

Internet(2010) Available: http://en.wikipedia.org/wiki/Won-Yo.

Internet(2010) Available: http://en.wikipedia.org/wiki/W%C5%8Dnhyo

Internet(2010) Available: http://en.wikipedia.org/wiki/Yang

Internet(2010) Available: http://en.wikipedia.org/wiki/%C5%9A%C5%ABnyat%C4%81

Internet(2010) Available: http://en.wikipedia.org/wiki/%C5%9Ar%C4%81vaka

Internet(2010) Available: http://ref.daum.net/item/11415305

Internet(2010) Available: http://www.budreview.com/news/articleView.html?idxno=627

Internet(2010) Available: http://www.lonelyplanet.com/south-korea/history

Internet(2010) Available: http://www.ymba.org/bns/bnsframe.htm

Internet(2010) Available: http://www.lonelyplanet.com/south-korea/history

Internet(2011) Available: http://blog.daum.net/cigong2500/7361176

Internet(2011) Available: http://www.budreview.com/news/article View.html?idxno=702

Index

A

Amittabha Buddha 104
amvamramhamkham 98
Asceticism 126
avarahakha 98
Avatamsaka Sūtra 165
Avatamsaka Sūtraism 165
Avidyā 111

B

Birojanabul(毘盧遮那佛) 89
Birojurn 183
Bodhi tree 126
bodhicittava 128
bodhisattvas 179
Bohhyun-bohsal 179
Bokwhangjurn 183
boundless interrelationships 170
Buddha Bliss Land 162
Buddha-nature 97
Bulgoksa Temple 164
Byupsung 103

C

Chaesangyoung 137

D

Daejurkgwhangjurn 183
Daekwangmaeyingjurn 183
Dharma 90
dharma-dhātu 154
Dharmakáya 89
Dharmakáya-Buddha 89
dhyāna-ism 157
Duckodang, Pubsung 103
dukkha 93

E

embodied Buddhas 134
enlightenment 111, 141
epiphany 109
esoteric holy words 133

G

gassho 98

great compassion 91

H
Haeinsa Temple 122
hetu 148
Hyetong 158

I
illumination 113
Impermanence 127
inward proof 140

J
jeambyen-myung 105
Jikwonin 107
jurnkak 183

K
karma 94
Kumkang Sūtra 107
kwangmusangmeal 105
Kwansheiomboshal 101
kāmaguna 96

L
lay disciple 151

M
Maitreya 158
meta-principle truth 152
meta-wind-circle 174
Mindfulness 102
Mt. Youngchook 101

N
Nirmanakáya 107
Nirmanakāya 136
Nirmanakāya-Buddha 115
nuengsungjungmu 105

O
oscillation 147

P
Pagoda-Buddha 123
philanthropy 131
prataya 148
Pure Bliss Land 111

R
reincarnation theory 176
Rhoshana-Buddha 183

S

Sabhava 156
Sabhā 90
Sabok Tale 176
Saekshimbuli 160
Sakyamuni 120
Sambhogakāya 135
Sambhokāya 124
Sammilgalgisokgilhyeun 149
self-realized Buddha 118
Simbonsaekmal 159
6 great unimpeded meta-elements 148
solidity 146
suddha 163
Sūtra 165

T

3 mystic meta-elements 149
3 secret activities 139
tiryagyoni-loka 153
Tongdosa Temple 124
Tusita-deva 176

U

unimpeded meta-elements 145

V

Vairocana's Dharma 91
vajrayāna 129
Variocana 165
virtue light 104

W

water-nature 147
west (*sukhāvatī*) 93
Whaomjurn 183
Wonhyoh 177
written holy words 133

Y

Yeoungkaksa Temple 185
Yukdaesamansammil 137

Editor's Profile ● **Jongil, Buddhist Monk**
Currently at the Temple of Bokyungsa(普鏡寺), Seoungnam, Korea
Born in Changyoung County, 1951
Resorted to Buddha as a Monk at Chunyoungsa Temple, 1967

Translator's Profile ● **Choonki, Park, Ph. D.**
E-mail: -ckp-@hanmail.net
Professor at Changwon Moonsung University(昌原文星大學), 1983~
Currently
Ph.D. in Literature at Choong-ang University, 1988
Visiting Scholar at Florida International University, 1990~1991
Teaching Professor at Shandong University of Finance, 2000~2001
Writing Way and Writing Well. Seoul: Hackmoon Press, 2006.
Teaching English to Children through Bilingualism. Seoul: Baeksan, 2010.

편저 ● 종일宗一

1967년 창녕 영축산 청련사靑蓮寺 입산
1973년 통도사 금강계단 월하月下 전계사 사미계 수지
1979년 통도사 전문강원 대교과大教科(22) 졸업
1980년 노천老天 월하 대종사로부터 건당
1981년 동국대학교 경영대학원 수료
1999년 대한민국 무형문화재 50호 범패 이수자

영어 ● 박춘기朴椿基

1952년 경남 창녕 출생
1988년 중앙대학교 대학원 영어영문학과 문학박사
1990년 미국 Florida International University 객원교수
2001년 중국 산동재정대학교 강의교환교수
현재 창원문성대학 교수

비로자나불

초판 1쇄 발행 2012년 4월 8일 | **초판 2쇄 발행** 2015년 1월 2일
편저 종일 | **영어** 박춘기 | **펴낸이** 김시열
펴낸곳 도서출판 운주사

(136-034) 서울시 성북구 동소문로 67-1 성심빌딩 3층
전화 (02) 926-8361 | 팩스 0505-115-8361

ISBN 978-89-5746-310-9 03220   값 12,000원
http://cafe.daum.net/unjubooks〈다음카페: 도서출판 운주사〉